36. How many of the following have you worn at the same time: corduroy pants, tweed jacket, cardigan sweater, striped socks, winning smile.

a. All 5 things (-10)

b. 4 things (-7)

c. 3 things (-5)

d. 2 things (-3)

e. I have not worn any of those things at the same time. (0)

f. I have not worn any of those things at any time. (1)

37. Of the following, which have you recently spent time in? (Check all that apply.)

a. The Air Force (3)

b. A back room in a Libyan government building (10)

c. The French winemaking region of Saint-Estephe (-1)

d. A Lady Gaga dance troupe (-4)

e. Jennifer Aniston (6)

38. What are you looking at?

a. This stupid quiz. (0)

b. Motherfucker, what are you looking at? (5)

-ANSWER KEY-

50 POINTS OR MORE: There are men and there are "men." You belong in both groups.

25 TO 49: You are three quarters of a "man."

1 TO 24: Five words: "Move before you are ready."—50 Cent, *The 50th Law*. In fact, read the whole book.

LESS THAN 0: Okay, let's start from the beginning. 'Sup.

32. Do you know your whereabouts on the night of March 29, 2011?

a. Yes (0)

b. No (0)

c. It wasn't me, man. (-3)

33. How do you pronounce this Scotch?

a. Brew-ik-lad-itch (5)

b. Brew-ich-luh ditch (5)

c. Brook-laddy (5)

d. Not even gonna try (-10)

For the correct pronunciation, see page 8.

34. IDENTIFY THESE NEW ICONS OF MANLINESS, ADD UP POINTS FOR EACH CORRECT ANSWER.

35. WORDSEARCH! Find all 10 words and then rearrange them to form a crucial question troubling you—and men like you all over America—at this very moment.

WORDSEARCH!

C	A	N	B	K	Y	O	U	P	K	L
B	E	L	I	E	V	E	H	W	Q	J
J	S	V	Q	D	F	W	S	X	U	I
P	Q	S	W	K	L	R	S	E	C	J
D	U	W	T	W	G	R	S	H	P	L
L	I	W	N	Q	D	L	K	O	D	P
H	R	G	H	W	V	Z	P	K	I	O
J	E	M	A	D	E	Y	F	W	C	V
F	B	D	W	G	O	B	D	N	M	N
Q	R	G	V	S	X	U	D	O	V	W
T	H	I	S	P	C	B	K	Q	N	M
V	K	L	W	F	U	C	K	I	N	G
W	O	R	D	S	E	A	R	C	H	?

If you found all 10 words, give yourself 5 points. If you were able to arrange the words into a sentence to form the crucial question, give yourself 5 more points

a. (0)   b. (-1)   c. (-3)   d. (-5)   e. (-9)

A. Messermeister Meridian Elite chef's knife. B. baby escarole C. KitchenAid Stand Mixer D. Allan Benton's famous bacon E. Guy Fieri holding a "No Can Beato This Taquito"

Esquire

How to Be a Man

A HANDBOOK OF ADVICE, INSPIRATION, AND OCCASIONAL DRINKING

HEARST BOOKS
New York

HEARST BOOKS
New York

An Imprint of Sterling Publishing
387 Park Avenue South
New York, NY 10016

ISBN 978-1-61837-077-8

Photograph and Illustration credits on page 186.

Distributed in Canada by Sterling Publishing
c/o Canadian Manda Group, 165 Dufferin Street
Toronto, Ontario, Canada M6K 3H6
Distributed in the United Kingdom by GMC Distribution Services
Castle Place, 166 High Street, Lewes, East Sussex, England BN7 1XU
Distributed in Australia by Capricorn Link (Australia) Pty. Ltd.
P.O. Box 704, Windsor, NSW 2756, Australia

For information about custom editions, special sales, and premium and
corporate purchases, please contact Sterling Special Sales at 800-805-5489 or
specialsales@sterlingpublishing.com.

Printed in United States of America

2 4 6 8 10 9 7 5 3 1

www.sterlingpublishing.com

CONTENTS

FOREWORD

A FEW YEARS AGO, we got a note from a 14-year-old who complained to us that his father had failed him. He claimed that everything he knew about being a man he'd learned from *Esquire*. It was one of the greatest letters (for us; maybe not so much for his dad). We took him under our wing and would occasionally advise him in matters of particular import. He's since made it safely to college, and although he did once send us a picture of himself wearing an ascot, we were proud to see him so proud.

As men, we know that being a man is as much about constantly learning as it is about sharing that which we have learned. One of the things *Esquire* has done more or less consistently for eighty years is offer advice. *Offer* is an important word. We don't so much *tell* people (men) how to live their lives; rather, we make suggestions. We (and lots of people we know) take note of what seems to have worked for them in their lives and we pass that information on.

Life, it turns out, is pretty much finding solutions to the situations in which we find ourselves. There is the getting-dressed situation. There is the attending-social-events situation. There is the relationship-with-the-most-important-and-beautiful-woman-in-the-world situation. There is the work situation. There is the drinking situation. There are shopping and grooming and sleeping and every other kind of situations. And we, *Esquire*, and our friends, have been there. It's not that we know the perfect way to navigate every situation. But we have some thoughts. We have a few suggestions.

This little book is a compilation of many of those thoughts.

In general, we feel that it is better to be generous in our dealings with other humans than not to be. We prize confidence and competence, as long as those attributes are expressed with a modicum of modesty. We believe that the best solution to just about every situation includes at least a little bit of humor. We believe that life is good and that we have the power to make it at least a little bit more enjoyable.

It's more than likely that you don't *need* this book. You've made it this far in life. But this book is not about need. I love it when a friend shows me a better way. I don't have to take his advice but it's good to have it in my repertoire.

A while back, I was breakfasting with Lyle Lovett. (Stop me if you've heard this one.) At one point, when Lyle's significant other returned to the table, Lyle stood up to greet her. Another friend asked Lyle why he did this. And Lyle said: "Because when you look like me, you need all the help you can get." We're all Lyle Lovett. Each of us can use all the help he can get.

David Granger
Editor in Chief, *Esquire*

CHAPTER ONE

ON DRINKING

WHAT I'VE LEARNED

I'm a fan of the margarita,
but never to extremes.
—GENERAL TOMMY FRANKS

You want a little more wine?
—MARIO BATALI

THE RULES

RULE NO. 131:
There is no shame in club soda
and cranberry juice.

RULE NO. 288:
No straws.

RULE NO. 301:
If the bartender has a mullet,
ordering a martini is probably
a bad idea.

HOW TO START THE NIGHT

GOALS ARE FINE, but when it comes to predetermined drinking limits, "two drinks" always means four drinks. Things to determine before committing to a new bar: Does the place have a television? Does it have two or more televisions? Is the bartender smiling? Is the bartender wearing a name tag? Are there specials listed on a sidewalk placard out front? Does it smell vaguely of cleaning products? Does the music seem ill-considered? Is it an Irish pub that offers fish tacos? (Correct answers: No. Only if it's a sports bar. Yes. No. No. No. No.)

If the bar is busy, stand behind a woman. Women don't seem to stick around as long as men—you'll get a seat faster. And maybe she's nice to talk to. Related: In a busy bar, wherever you're standing is the best place to be. Also, there is no reserving of seats for a companion who has not yet arrived.

For the first round, always "cheers," clink of the glass, a look in the eye. Unless you're alone. If you're alone, then do not do this.

If you're at a place that seems to take a long time making drinks, order your second drink before you finish your first. (But after you've started it.) If you are at a place that seems to take a long time making drinks and the drink that you ordered is not very good, then make your second drink a beer. Or find a more tolerable bar.

A few things to talk about with the bartender while you're waiting for someone to arrive: the strangest-looking bartending implement he's using, how he's been, how tasty this drink is, muddling, his least favorite drink to make, the worst customer he's ever had, mustache care, the likelihood that anyone has ever in the history of the bar asked for a pour from that bottle of Marie Brizard on the shelf back there.

HOW TO END THE NIGHT

THINGS THAT YOU might be talking about that are pretty solid indications that the night should end: your crushing loneliness, how much love you have to share, how wonderful your dog is, the guy staring back at you in the mirror and what he could've been if only somebody had given him a chance, Dad, how much money you make, new worries associated with rising CO_2 levels, how you have to go take a leak, what happened yesterday.

If you plan on coming back soon, wildly over tip.

Questions to ask yourself before leaving: Might I need to use the men's room? Is this my date? Do I really need to finish that drink? Might I benefit from some water? Where am I? Where is my home? Did I sign the credit-card receipt? Who was Pappy Van Winkle, really? Nightcap?

In terms of how to leave, you could, you know, leave. Leaving is fairly definitive. You could leave without saying goodbye, which is an "Irish exit"—it works only when everyone's drunk. After exiting the restroom, you just walk past the bar and out the door. No one will notice, no one will care. In the morning, they'll probably think you said goodbye. In general, it's better to leave before you'd like to. Because "before you'd like to" is actually "right when you should." Sliding scale.

That's not your umbrella.

THE STAGES OF DRINKING

		DRINKS HAD
STAGE 1	**DETERMINATION** Marked by: Thinking about having a drink, being asked if you would like to have a drink, ruminating on the possibilities that drink may afford you, and then determining to have a drink. And smiling.	**0**
STAGE 2	**REQUISITION** Marked by: Getting yourself to where drinks are, confidently ordering something you know you like or that the bartender recommends, assessing your surroundings, sipping. And grinning.	**0–.5**
STAGE 3	**CONSUMPTION** Marked by: Drinking, conversing, making plans, telling a story, giving advice, recounting an experience. And chuckling.	**1–4**
STAGE 4	**CONSUMPTION** Marked by: Drinking but faster, talking but louder, making plans but vaguer, telling an almost-compelling story. And chortling.	**3–6**
STAGE 5	**??????** Marked by: Sentences that begin with the phrase "I thought she…"; an imagined force field that makes your actions and utterances visible only to those people you are looking at directly; indiscriminate use of the expression "Woo."	**?**
STAGE 6	**REFLECTION** Marked by: A period of hours, days, and, in some cases, years in which the events of Stages 1 to 5 are shaped, molded, grappled with, and beaten down, but ultimately cherished and used as inspiration for the next Stage 1. And smiling.	**0**

HOW TO

BE ALONE AT A BAR

1. Keep your phone in your pocket.
2. Equip yourself with a pretty good answer to the question "What are you shaking your head for?"
3. Shake your head for longer than is normal.
4. When someone asks why, have a conversation.

ORDER YOUR SECOND TO LAST DRINK

1. "Water, please."
2. Drink water.
3. "Another bourbon."
4. Drink water.
5. Sip bourbon.
6. Drink water.

DISCREETLY WEEP

1. Order martini.
2. Say that you forgot you were allergic to vermouth. "Damn vermouth."
3. Weep.
OR
1. Order martini.
2. Spill martini on your face so that tears are masked by gin.
3. Weep.
OR
1. Order martini.
2. Bring tablet computer extremely close to face. "Checking my emails."
3. Weep.

THE DO'S AND DON'TS

OF A CROWDED BAR

Wait to order near the taps. It's where the bartender will most often be.

◆

Overtip on the first round. Your bartender will remember you when you come back.

Brief eye contact only. He'll get to you.

◆

No matter your hunger level, never eat garnishes out of the fruit tray.

◆

If this is 1964 and you're celebrating O'Malley's retirement from the force, then, and only then, should you yell for the "barkeep."

◆

Know where you are. Which is to say, don't order an old-fashioned at a sports bar, a beer at a cocktail bar, or a Long Island iced tea at a beer bar.

◆

In fact, never order a Long Island iced tea.

◆

Putting a coaster on your drink buys you five minutes, tops. And you can only do it once an hour. If that's troubling, maybe you should stop smoking so much.

SPECTRUM OF
BAR NOMENCLATURE

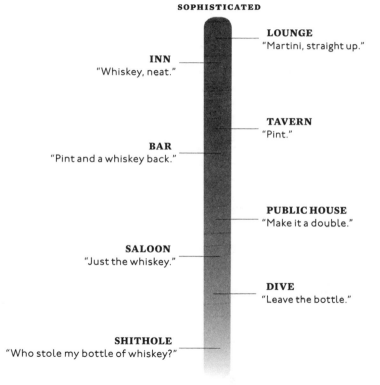

SOPHISTICATED

LOUNGE
"Martini, straight up."

INN
"Whiskey, neat."

TAVERN
"Pint."

BAR
"Pint and a whiskey back."

PUBLIC HOUSE
"Make it a double."

SALOON
"Just the whiskey."

DIVE
"Leave the bottle."

SHITHOLE
"Who stole my bottle of whiskey?"

UNSOPHISTICATED

THE AMERICAN MAN'S GUIDE
TO THE PRONUNCIATION OF SCOTCHES

⬆

AN CNOK
AH-nock

AUCHENTOSHAN
AUK-en-TOSH-en

BRUICHLADDICH
brook-LADDY

BUNNAHAB HAIN
boo-na-HAHB-en

THE BALVENIE
bol-VAINNY

BOWMORE
ba-more

CA OL ILA
coo-LEE-la

CARDHU
car-DEW

DALWHINNIE
dal-WHINNIE

GLENFARCLAS
glen-FARK-lass

GLENFIDDICH
glen-FIDD-ik

GLENLIVET
glen-LIV-it

GLENKINCHIE
glen-KINCH-ee

GLENMORANGIE
glen-MORE-an-jee

GLENROTHES
glen-ROTH-is

⬇

⬆

HIGHLAND PARK
hai-lund PARK

JURA
JOO-ra

LAGAVULIN
la-ga-VOOL-in

LAPHROAIG
la-FROYG

MACALLAN
muck-AL-un

OBAN
OA-bun

TALISKER
TAL-is-kur

TOMINTOUL
tom-in-TOWEL

THE MASTER LIST OF
HANGOVER REMEDIES

THE POISON	THE SYMPTOMS	THE REMEDY
BEER	The grains and yeast contained in beer lead to bloating and diarrhea.	Alka-Seltzer Plus. The carbonation soothes your nausea, while the aspirin takes care of the headache.
RED WINE	The tannins lead to sharp, migraine-esque headaches.	Gatorade and aspirin. The aspirin eases headaches while the Gatorade helps replace the fluids you've lost around the brain.
WHITE WINE	The sugar content in some white wines can trigger dehydration and headaches.	Rehydrating with some water over the course of the day and an ibuprofen for the headache.
DARK LIQUORS	These contain congeners, substances that when metabolized can lead to intense nausea.	A whiskey and lemonade (preferably with homemade lemonade). Lemon stimulates digestion while whiskey decreases withdrawal symptoms. Or: See *red wine*.
CARBONATED MIXED DRINKS	The carbonation causes you to absorb the alcohol faster and increases the likelihood of dehydration.	See *red wine*.

SIGNS YOU'RE IN A BAD BAR

THE BARTENDERS ARE WEARING NAME TAGS.

AND THEY SEEM VERY EXCITED TO SEE YOU.

THAT UNEASY FEELING YOU FELT BEFORE YOU WALKED IN
ISN'T DIMINISHING NOW THAT YOU'RE DRUNK.

JAGER SHOT MACHINE.

"MAY I SEE YOUR ID?"

THE PLACE SMELLS LIKE IT'S RECENTLY BEEN DISINFECTED.

IT SEEMS "KID-FRIENDLY."

IN FACT, THERE ARE BABIES—BABIES RIGHT THERE IN THE BAR.

THE BAR'S NAME IS A PLURAL NOUN
FOR SOMETHING PLEASANT (E.G. WHISPERS).

THE BAR'S NAME ENDS IN Z (E.G., WHISPERZ).

YOU'RE THE ONLY ONE THERE.

CHAPTER TWO

ON FOOD

WHAT I'VE LEARNED

Food is about meeting people and
sharing the experience.
—LUDO LEFEBVRE

There is nothing worse
than grilled vegetables.
—JULIA CHILD

THE RULES

RULE NO. 115:
There is no shame in the peanut
butter sandwich.

RULE NO. 181:
Never cook with wine that you
wouldn't want to drink.

RULE NO. 211:
You cut the fat, you cut the flavor.

THREE TOOLS

**EVERY MAN
OBVIOUSLY NEEDS**

NONE OF WHICH IS A
PREASSORTED TWELVE-PIECE
COOKWARE SET

| ALL-CLAD ROASTING PAN | STAUB DUTCH OVEN WITH LID | LODGE LOGIC CAST-IRON SKILLET |

DON'T RUIN AN expensive roast with a cheap pan. Only quality construction can take the heat without scorching (creating hot spots that cause uneven cooking) or warping (causing all the fat to collect in one corner), so get yourself a heavy-gauge stainless-steel roasting pan with solid cast handles. Just measure your oven first. This pan needs two inches of space all around it for airflow.

A DUTCH OVEN is an all-round pot for braising, stewing, and pot-roasting. Minimal hands-on time coaxes maximum flavor from even the most inexpensive cuts of meat (like brisket and shoulder). Made in Alsace, France, by a family company dating to 1892, the Staub cocotte's lid has spikes on the underside, like stalactites, so steam condenses and drips back into the pot for self-basting.

THERE'S NO GREATER symbol of the American kitchen that the almighty cast-iron skillet, and there's no better cast-iron skillet than one made by Lodge. Crafted to retain even heat whether you're searing, braising, frying, or even baking, the innovative "Logic" line is pre-seasoned to create a natural nonstick surface and glossy heirloom patina right out of the box.

THREE TOOLS

**NO MAN KNOWS
HE NEEDS**

YOU WON'T UNDERSTAND HOW
ESSENTIAL THESE ARE UNTIL
THE FIRST TIME YOU USE THEM

ALL-CLAD SAUTEUSE	ALL-CLAD BUTTER WARMER	WEAREVER JELLY-ROLL PAN

A MARRIAGE BETWEEN a skillet and a saucepan, wide enough for sautéing, deep enough for poaching and frying, and has a slightly rounded underside that gives room for adding liquid. The domed lid allows one-pot cooking for larger cuts of meat, and the two heatproof handles make it easier and safer to lift the full pan off the stove.

LIKE ANY GREAT tool, this two-cup pot, originally designed to melt and clarify butter, has many uses. Stainless steel and bonded with tri-ply construction so it won't buckle, it's ideal for warming syrup, infusing oil, heating sauce or soup (without evaporation over a larger cooking surface), or even making a little rice.

IT LOOKS LIKE a cookie sheet, but its sturdy construction (no warping) and even heating properties mean this pan can do so much more: roast vegetables, toast croutons, or even serve as a makeshift roaster for large cuts of meat that don't throw off liquid (like a tenderloin or a ham) or whole fish.

MASTER OF YOUR GRILL

A THREE-STEP GUIDE TO OWNING THE FIRE

THERE'S A REASON MEN STAND GUARD OVER THEIR GRILLS: Fire is alive, wind is unpredictable, adjustments are always necessary. Plus, it makes you look knowledgeable and very busy. Since barbecuing is often a group affair that involves more than one thing cooking, it takes vigilant timing as well as a tolerance for preferences. You are more short-order cook than chef, handling requests for blackened dogs, rare steaks, and chicken that's "not too burny." For maximum grill efficiency, sanity, and success, the first step is to learn to work your grill in three cooking zones: hot, medium, and low. Then you can grill anything. Steaks. Chops. Corn. Bacon. Clams. F*cking pineapple. Anything.

> **TIP: TOUCH YOUR FOOD.** *No matter how sophisticated your grilling rig, you're still cooking over a primitive heat source. Use your instincts: Consider recipe timing a guideline and rely on how something looks, smells, and even feels (when you poke it with your finger) to determine if it's ready.*

THE HEAT ZONES AND WHAT TO DO WITH THEM

LOW HEAT (covered grill)	MODERATE HEAT	BIG HEAT

INDIRECT HEAT
For Cooking All The Way Through

Large roasts • Anything wrapped in bacon • Plank-roasted fish • Tougher cuts of meat (like brisket) • Ribs • Whole chickens, spatch-cocked (cut so they lay flat—ask your butcher)

MEDIUM HEAT
For Even Cooking

Skin-on chicken pieces • Pork chops • Sausages • Corn on the cob (in husk) • Fish, including shellfish (lay right on the grill— they're done when they open)

HIGH HEAT
For Searing

Thin steaks • Vegetables (slice 'em thin) • Burgers (medium rare) • Kabobs (may need to be moved to moderate fire to finish cooking) • Pounded chicken cutlets

PLACE A METAL DRIP PAN IN YOUR LOW-HEAT (NO-FIRE ZONE). KEEP SOME WATER IN IT THROUGHOUT COOKING. THIS KEEPS DRIPPINGS FROM BURNING AND ADDS MOISTURE SO LARGE CUTS OF MEAT WON'T DRY OUT.

8 THINGS
NO ONE EVER
TEACHES
YOU ABOUT GRILLING

by Steven Raichlen

❶ GET THE GRILL SCREAMING HOT

For steaks, chops, and burgers, hold your hand three inches above the grill grate and start counting, "One Mississippi, two Mississippi, etc." If "ouch" comes at two or three Mississippi, your grill is properly preheated.

❷ . . . AND SQUEAKY CLEAN

Always clean your grate immediately before and after cooking, using a long-handled stiff wire brush. In a pinch, you can scour the grate with a ball of crumpled aluminum foil held in tongs.

❸ . . . AND WELL-LUBRICATED

Use a tightly folded paper towel dipped in vegetable oil

or a chunk of bacon fat held at the end of your tongs to oil the grate before you put on the food. Or do as Israeli grill masters do: Impale half an onion on the end of a barbecue fork. Dip the onion in oil and rub it across the bars of the grate.

❹ EDIBLE SKEWERS
Skewer meat or seafood on sprigs of fresh rosemary (great for lamb), cinnamon sticks (great for pork and peaches), or lemongrass stalks (great for chicken, shrimp, and swordfish).

❺ THE BEER BOTTLE BASTING BRUSH
Open a longneck bottle of beer, cover the mouth of the bottle with your thumb, then shake it. Gradually slide back your thumb and direct the resulting stream of beer on the meat.

❻ THE FOUR-FINGER THERMOMETER
Form the "okay" sign, touching the tip of your thumb to the tip of your forefinger. The pad of flesh at the base of your thumb will feel soft and squishy—

exactly the same way a rare steak feels when you poke the top with your forefinger. Now move the tip of your thumb to the tip of your middle finger: That's medium-rare. Thumb to the tip of your ring finger: medium. Thumb to pinkie: well-done.

❼ COOK ON THE COALS
Lay sweet potatoes, onions, and even corn in the husk directly on the embers. Roast, turning with tongs, until the skins are coal black. When you scrape off the burned skin, the vegetable inside will be supernaturally sweet and smoky.

❽ THE INDIRECT METHOD
This will solve several potential problems: Large or tough foods have time to cook through without burning. Fatty foods don't cause flare-ups. And because you measure the cooking time in hours, you don't have to worry about split-second timing. To set up a charcoal grill for indirect grilling, light the coals

(ideally, lump charcoal) in a chimney starter and dump or rake them into two mounds at opposing sides of the grill. Place an aluminum drip pan in the center. (The pan serves to catch the dripping fat, while obliging you to configure your fire the correct way for indirect grilling.) Next, place the food to be grilled in the center of the grill, away from coals, over the drip pan. Close the lid and adjust the vent holes (more air, hotter fire; less air, cooler fire) to obtain the desired temperature — usually moderate (300 to 350 degrees) for roasting whole poultry or pork shoulder. The ultimate meat for indirect grilling is that barbecue icon of the Carolinas: pork shoulder (sometimes called Boston butt). The relatively high heat (higher than the true low and slow barbecue of the American South) produces succulent meat with a crackling-crisp crust, while deftly eliminating the risk of flare-ups.

HOW TO **MAKE PANCAKES**

From Scratch

SERVES FOUR

Have you never cooked breakfast for children—or drunks? Been a Boy Scout? Have you never had an attractive woman spend the night in your bed? There are few things an American man must know how to cook, but pancakes are one of them. The good news is they're easy—almost as easy from scratch as from a box mix. Here's how:

INGREDIENTS
2 cups all-purpose flour
2 ½ tsp baking powder
½ tsp salt
1 egg, beaten lightly
1 ½ cups milk
2 tbsp butter, melted

• Sift together first three ingredients (to prevent lumps).

• In a separate bowl, mix egg and milk, then add it to flour mix, stirring until just smooth. Then stir in butter.

• If you want to mix it up, throw in blueberries, a tiny dice of apple, or bits of banana.

• Grease a griddle or non-stick pan with cooking spray or a little vegetable oil.

• Heat pan on medium for about ten minutes.

• Pour batter to form pancakes of whatever size you like.

• Cook first side until bubbles form on top, about three minutes; then flip and cook other side until it, too, is brown, about two minutes.

• Serve immediately with butter and syrup or hold briefly in warm oven.

HOW TO MAKE EGGS
FOUR WAYS

❶
SCRAMBLED

Crack three eggs into a bowl. Add a dash of salt and pepper and a tablespoon of milk. Whisk till extra fluffy, about twenty seconds. Heat pan with butter over medium heat and add eggs. Once they begin to solidify (about twenty seconds), start to softly scramble with a spatula. After another twenty seconds or so, when the eggs are two thirds of the way cooked but still wet, move pan to a cold burner and stir until barely cooked through.

❷
BAKED

Place a six-inch cast-iron skillet (lightly coated with olive oil) in oven and preheat to 375 degrees. Once oven is fully heated, remove skillet and add tomatoes or asparagus or bacon. Sausage or day-old brisket is even better. Brown lightly for a couple minutes, then crack in two eggs and add a dash of salt and pepper. Place back in oven for about five minutes.

❸
POACHED

Bring a pot of water to a light boil, then add one capful of white vinegar. Crack an egg into a cup. Lightly stir the water to get it moving in one direction, then carefully pour egg from cup into the center of the pot. After about two minutes, retrieve egg with a slotted spoon and drain on a paper towel.

❹
SUNNY-SIDE UP

Crack eggs into a generously buttered pan over low-medium heat. (If you have leftover bacon grease, that's even better.) Once whites are formed, about three minutes, spoon some excess butter or fat onto the yolk to lightly cook the top for one minute. Remove once the edges of the egg begin to get crispy.

HOW TO **CARVE A TURKEY**

TOOLS: *8-INCH CHEF'S KNIFE,*
12-INCH SERRATED CARVING KNIFE

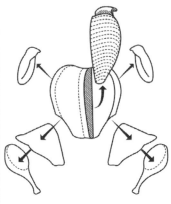

❶ PLACE THE TURKEY on a cutting board and remove the legs and thighs: While pulling the thigh back away from the breast, use your chef's knife to make small, rapid cuts into the skin, eventually exposing the joint. Then pull the entire leg-and-thigh portion away from the bird with enough force to crack the joint. Cut all the way through and remove the leg, and then do the same with the wings.

❷ ONCE YOU'VE SEPARATED the legs and wings, the drumsticks should easily pull away from the thighs. Set the drumsticks aside. Remove the meat from the thighs by scraping it from the bone with the chef's knife. Once it's off the bone, slice the meat with your chef's knife. (Leave the drumsticks and wings intact. Because they look cool.)

❸ FOR THE BREAST, make one long lateral cut with a chef's knife along the side until you reach the rib cage.

❹ MAKE ANOTHER CUT from the sternum down along the rib cage until you've reached the location of the first cut. Remove the whole thing (it should resemble one fourth of a football cut lengthwise) and place it on the cutting board.

❺ WITH THE SERRATED CARVING KNIFE, cut the breast into ½-inch-thick slices, careful to keep the skin on each slice. Serve.

HOW TO **FILLET A FISH**

TOOLS: *FILLET KNIFE,*
FILLET GLOVES

STEP 1 Rinse the dead fish using ocean or purified water—tap makes it taste funky — and if you're going to cook it with the skin on, descale it using the dull edge of the fillet knife, scraping against the grain until the surface is smooth.

STEP 2 Place the fish on its side on a sturdy table or board. Insert your knife near the top of the dorsal fin, just behind the head, stopping when you hit backbone. Then slice along the dorsal fin, holding the blade edge tight against the backbone, until you reach the tail. Turn the fish over on its other side and repeat.

STEP 3 Starting just behind the head, slide your blade part of the way up the rib cage (at a slight upward angle) and cut through the skin while pulling the fillet away from the fish. Do not cut the skin where it is attached to the tail. Flip the fillet over so it lies flat on top of the tail (skin side down) and at the edge of your table.

STEP 4 With your knife parallel to the top of the table, slide the blade along the bottom of the fillet using downward pressure and separate the meat from the skin. Remove as much of the red meat as possible without destroying the white meat (i.e., the part you eat). Repeat with the other side.

HOW TO **MAKE A PAN SAUCE**

For Any Meat

❶ CUT SHALLOTS OR ONIONS into thin slices or small dice. Add to the hot pan after removing meat. They will release moisture, loosening flavorful bits of meat ("fond") from the pan. This is the first deglaze. A pat of butter helps, too—the milk solids will caramelize and attach themselves to the fond.

❷ ADD SOME CUT-UP VEGETABLES, but nothing that takes long to cook or the sauce will evaporate and your protein will get cold. Try mushrooms, jarred artichoke hearts, or olives.

❸ THE SECOND DEGLAZE IS WITH LIQUID: first some wine, then some stock (or even water). This time, scrape the pan with a wooden spoon to get all the tasty bits incorporated into the sauce.

❹ SWIRL IN SOME BUTTER, maybe a tablespoon. Use a spoon or pick up the pan and move it in quick circles over the burner. Done.

HOW TO TIE

A BUTCHER'S SLIPKNOT

STEP 1

Wrap the string around the roast with the ends up.

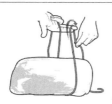

STEP 2

Holding your right hand like a toy gun, grab the bottom end of the string with your ring and pinkie fingers. Wrap the top end all the way around your pointer and middle fingers (the barrel of the gun).

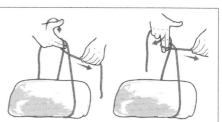

STEP 3

Twist your hand to aim the gun at the roast. Spread your index and middle fingers, creating a loop in the string between them. Bring the top end through the loop.

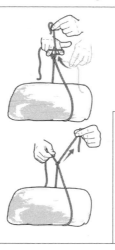

STEP 4

Feed the top string through the loop, then pull it up through the loop with your left hand while pulling back on the bottom string with your right.

STEP 5

Slip the knot into place and trim ends.

DINNER FOR TEN

*How to throw a medium-sized dinner party
without a hitch*

They've arrived! Now get a drink in your guests' hands quickly. Could be champagne, could be a cold beer, could be a martini—something. There is no shame in offering a selection of, say, three drinks, and that's it, and you should make sure to have something for non-drinkers other than water and Diet Coke. (Seltzer with fruit garnishes is good.) Also, there's a reason it's called a cocktail hour—people drink too much and get too hungry if it lasts much longer.

Don't overstuff people with too many apps or munchies upon arrival—one or two options (including a well-stocked antipasti plate they can graze on) should be plenty.

When inviting your guests, ask if they have any dietary restrictions and plan your meal accordingly. And never, ever try to pull off a dish you've never made before. Keep it simple and remember that just because you're into, say, Mongolian-Brazilian fusion right now doesn't mean your guests will agree.

If you're entertaining a senator, that's one thing. But for normal humans, cook stuff people like to eat. Follow the well-worn path set by restaurants: a light salad, a bread basket, the main course (a protein, a starch, and a vegetable), and a dessert with coffee.

Keep the place setting simple. If people want baby forks and eight different wineglasses, they can go to a restaurant. For home, it's two forks (salad and dinner), two plates (dinner and bread), two glasses (water and wine), a knife, a spoon, and a napkin.

Be aware of how much alcohol you drink. Getting too drunk at your own party has consequences, not the least of which is that you'll overcook the food.

Buy at least one bottle of wine per person, and when in doubt, buy more red than white. (White-wine drinkers generally don't mind switching to red; red drinkers generally do mind switching to white.)

Opt for low light, but not so low that things devolve into an orgy—unless that's

what you're going for—and if you go with candles (always a good move), make sure the candles are low enough that they're not in anyone's field of vision.

Pick a mellow and interesting but unobtrusive playlist—try mixing contemporary, low-key rock (i.e., the XX, Grizzly Bear) with your standard-issue Bowies and Lou Reeds.

Keep a bottle of red open at either end of the table at all times so people can help themselves; keep a bottle of white chilled by your end of the table and refill people's glasses as needed.

Boy-girl-boy-girl is still the best option for arranged seating, and when in doubt, put couples next to each other. (That way, if a man is next to an annoying stranger, he has his wife to talk to; if, however, he's next to a fascinating, beautiful stranger, his wife can fend for herself.)

HOW TO COOK WITH

WHAT YOU'RE DRINKING

THINK OF ALCOHOL AS AN EXTRACT, MEANT TO GIVE YOU CONCENTRATED FLAVOR, NOT A BUZZ. GENERALLY, THE HIGHER THE ALCOHOL CONTENT, THE LATER IN THE PROCESS YOU ADD IT. **NOTE:** WHEN ADDING SPIRITS, PULL THE PAN AWAY FROM THE HEAT AND DON'T POUR STRAIGHT FROM THE BOTTLE. SO AS NOT TO START A FIRE.

BOURBON	• Add to barbecue sauce or maple syrup. • Mix with sweet potatoes and baked beans. • Drop in stews or braises (especially with chilis) • Deglaze a pan to make a quick butter sauce for steak or pork chops
VODKA	• Its light, clean taste pairs well with fish and poultry. • And tomatoes (e.g., a Bloody Mary, pasta sauce). • Mix with salsa to make a marinade for grilled chicken. • Splash into cocktail sauce.
LAGER	• Hops can turn bitter when beer is reduced, so use in low-heat applications. • Include in batters (like those for fried fish) and marinades (especially for game). • Dilute stews, chilis, and braises.
WHITE OR RED WINE	• Mix into braises, chilis, and stews. • Deglaze a pan to make sauce for fish, poultry, or meat. • Add to marinades—the acidity helps break down proteins and tenderize tough cuts of meat.
VERMOUTH	• Fortified wine is stronger than standard white (so use less). • Enhances shellfish dishes like mussels with chorizo and linguine with clam sauce.

CHAPTER THREE

ON WOMEN

WHAT I'VE LEARNED

It's not women who are tough.
It's life.
—ELLIOT GOULD

If God made anything better
than women, I think He kept
it for Himself.
—KRIS KRISTOFFERSON

THE RULES

RULE NO. 420:
Women named after a month of the
year are usually frisky.

RULE NO. 448:
Women like a man who likes women
who like to eat.

RULE NO. 461:
Women whose names end with the
letter "i" are more promiscuous.

THE LANGUAGE OF WOMEN

"IS THAT WHAT YOU'RE WEARING?"
A question to which the only acceptable answer is "Not anymore."

"EVERYTHING HAPPENS FOR A REASON"
A phrase of comfort and consolation, intended to convey that even bad things will one day work out for the best. Typically delivered by someone in no way qualified to give such a reassurance.

"HONESTLY"
A means to emphasize the import of a statement or question. Is not necessarily related to truthfulness.

"WHAT ARE YOU THINKING ABOUT?"
"Say something nice about me."

"NOTHING"
When used as a declarative statement and pronounced at slow or rapid speeds, translates to "definitely something." When pronounced at more moderate speeds, translates faithfully to "nothing."

"BOYS"
❶ Males who have not yet reached adulthood.
❷ Males who have already reached adulthood.

"CUTE"
❶ Aesthetically pleasing, in a broad sense. Includes, but is not limited to, babies, puppies, and shoes. ❷ May also be used to refer to considerate, thoughtful behavior. Like the time you surprised her with a cute puppy.

RESPONSE GENERATOR

SITUATIONS THAT MAY ARISE WITH THE WOMAN IN YOUR LIFE,
AND HOW TO HANDLE THEM.

	NEW RELATIONSHIP	LONG-TERM RELATIONSHIP
SHE SNEEZES	"Bless you."	"Bless you."
SHE SAYS "I LOVE YOU"	"I really care about you." Anything but "Already?"	"Love you, too." Never: "Still?"
HER DOG DIES	Hugs, space, donation to the local shelter, or maybe just a stuffed animal	Hugs, space, flowers (gardenias are nice), framed picture of the dog, a new dog (when she's ready)
SHE BREAKS WIND AT A COCKTAIL PARTY	Pretend it didn't happen. Take her to get another drink.	Heroically take credit.
SHE WANTS TO HAVE BRUNCH	Pick a sweet place and take her to brunch.	Tell her to have a good time.

COOL

THE REACTION GUIDE

···

PROPER RESPONSES TO UNCOMFORTABLE SITUATIONS

SHE'S GIVING YOU THE SILENT TREATMENT →	Say, "I love you" and smile innocently.
WHERE'S DINNER? →	"You know what would be so great? That (*fantastic dish here*) that you made a couple of weeks ago."
SHE'S YELLING →	Find out at whom she's yelling. If it's someone else, let her yell. If it's you, say, "Let's have a drink and talk about it."
HER CHIN IS QUIVERING →	Immediate hug.
SHE'S STILL GETTING READY →	Remember that she just wants to look her best.
SHE'S RUNNING A TEMPERATURE →	Two Tylenol and fluids.
SHE WON'T HAVE SEX WITH YOU →	Give her a back rub (see page 34), kiss her neck.
HER FRIEND IS EXTREMELY ATTRACTIVE →	Avoid direct eye contact.
SHE WON'T RETURN YOUR CALLS →	Move on.

IN BRIEF:

THE ART OF TALKING

A handy register of location-specific conversation with unknown women

	AWKWARD	PASSABLE	GOOD
AT THE OFFICE	The boss can be a real dick sometimes, huh?	What's for lunch?	Hi, (*Then continue to your desk.*)
ON AN AIRPLANE	Where you headed?	Is that book any good?	May I help you with that?
AT A BALL GAME	I like their costumes.	[*Home team*] always finds a way to blow it.	May I buy you a $9 beer?
AT THE DENTIST	I heard him say you hadn't been flossing. That's not something to take lightly.	I only cried a little this time.	[Silence. Brief smile.]
AT CHURCH	You buy this baloney?	Peace be with you.	And also with you.

HOW TO **COMPLIMENT A WOMAN**

IT IS AS MUCH A SKILL AS IT IS A NECESSITY.
A FEW RULES AND EXAMPLES TO GUIDE YOUR WAY. ADAPT. REPEAT.

You can say that her hair is an improvement but not so much of an improvement as to imply that you didn't like it before.
TRY:
"I like what you're doing with your hair."

As basic as it sounds, women love to hear that a color looks great on them.
TRY:
"That color looks really nice on you."

When complimenting her chest or ass, try to avoid sounding lascivious.
TRY:
"That color looks really nice on you."

Never harp. It seems disingenuous.
TRY:
"Love your hair. When's dinner?"

Your niece looks cute or pretty. Your wife looks gorgeous, stunning, beautiful or amazing.
TRY:
"You look [any of the words above]."

Nothing says sincerity more than the look on your face. Either that or a well-placed expletive.
TRY:
"You look f*cking amazing."

When in doubt, go simple.
TRY:
"Wow."

HOW TO
SLOW DANCE
WITH HER

- **HAVE A DRINK** or two.

- **LEAD HER** to the floor with your elbow (or hand) and don't let go until you start dancing.

- **POSITION HER** so there is an imaginary straight line going from her sternum to the inside of your right shoulder. This will stagger your bodies and allow room for error.

- **PLACE YOUR RIGHT HAND** flat on the small of her back and hold your left out to the side, at chest level, inviting her right hand to join yours. Your hands should be

interlocking c's, not intertwined.

- **SPACING IS KEY.** A good three to six inches, say. The goal is intimacy that still allows her to move freely. There

should be a relaxed, comfortable bend in both elbows. Your joined arms—forearms to elbows—should resemble the bow of a ship.

- **MOVE CLOCKWISE.** Your right foot is the anchor. Shift all your weight to one foot, then every time you hit the "one" on the four-count beat, give or take, shift your weight to the other. And so on.

- **SLOW DOWN.**

- **NO DIPPING.** Because this is when injuries happen.

- **EYE CONTACT.**

THE BETTER BACK RUB

YOU HAVE TO KNOW YOUR ANATOMY. AND LISTEN.

I. THE TRAPEZIUS

The first thing is oil. Any good massage oil from a health-food store will work. Some favorites from around the home: jojoba or grape-seed. Make sure that the recipient is in a comfortable seated position in front of you. Place your hands on her shoulders and grab the trapezius— the big muscle that leads from the neck to the shoulders, the one everybody loves to have rubbed. Shake it a little bit back and forth. Squeeze it, rub it. Push up against the neck a little bit but move down toward the shoulders. Don't be afraid of using too much pressure. If your partner moans or says, "That's the spot," stick with it.

2. THE SHOULDER BLADES

Then move on to the shoulder blades. Pay particular attention to the space between the shoulder blades and the vertebral column. Use your fingertips to rub back and forth between the vertebral column and the shoulder blade. Be vigorous. And whatever you're massaging when she says, "That's the spot," stay on that spot.

3. THE VERTEBRAL COLUMN

Run your thumbs down each side of the spinal column. Push them into the back and move all the way down without touching bone. Never massage bone. Go up and down one side and up and down the opposite side.

HOW TO **BUY A WOMAN CLOTHING**

TOOLS: *CREDIT CARD, WOMAN'S CLOTHING SIZE*

I. Don't.

HOW TO **APPLY SUNSCREEN**

TO A WOMAN'S BACK

❶

WAIT until you are asked.
Don't stand around with sunscreen on your hand.

❷

DO NOT APPLY the sunscreen directly to her back.
Instead, put it on your hands and begin rubbing on her back,
making sure not to miss any spots.

❸

KEEP TALKING while you do it.
There's nothing creepier than someone silently rubbing your back.
Ask if you missed anything.

❹

LEAVE THE FRONT to her.
Unless she asks.

HOW TO GIVE A FOOT MASSAGE

❶

Prepare the feet with massage oil by first applying it to your hands and then in broad strokes over the feet.

❷

Then, with one hand on top of the foot and the other on the bottom of the foot, rub in circles.

❸

Next, place both thumbs on top of the foot, with fingers wrapped around and under the foot's bones. Apply pressure up and down the length of the top of the foot, from ankle to toes.

❹

Use a similar technique for the bottom of the foot: Firmly push down the center line of the sole with both thumbs. Try applying pressure for ten seconds on five different points from the heel to the tip of the toes.

❺

Ask how good it was. Collect your reward.

HOW TO **MAKE A DRINK**

JUST FOR HER

by David Wondrich

SOME WOMEN ALWAYS KNOW just what they want to drink. Some don't. Some want a suggestion, a surprise, something light and delicious and just for them. Something like the Rose Cocktail, a Parisian favorite from the 1920s that turns vermouth and dry cherry brandy into something very special indeed.

STIR WELL WITH ICE:

2 oz dry vermouth
1 oz imported kirschwasser
1 tsp raspberry syrup or Chambord

Strain into a chilled cocktail glass and garnish with a cherry.

PHONE-GREETING TRANSLATOR

HI! →	She likes you!
HEY, YOU →	She's been thinking about you.
WELL, HELL-O →	She's been thinking about sleeping with you.
HEY →	Impossible to tell.
HI THERE →	She's probably not interested.
YO →	She'd love to stay friends.
WHATTUP! →	She's sixteen.
WHO IS THIS? →	She doesn't know who you are.

HOW TO HANDLE A
HOT WOMAN

Solutions for a woman who is not enjoying the heat

SPICY FOOD: Is she hungry? Are you near your kitchen or that of a person who charges to cook things in his? Counterintuitive as it may seem, spicy food causes you to sweat without raising body temperature. That sweat will evaporate and cool her skin.

TEA: Put a couple of used tea bags in an airtight container in the fridge to cool. Take them out and place them near the pulse points on her inner wrists. They'll help her feel cooler, and, if you had the foresight to pick peppermint tea, will have the refreshing sensation of menthol.

ALOE VERA: Lotion with aloe vera (or a stalk from the plant) instantly lowers her skin temperature. Especially if you thought ahead and stored it in the fridge. You know, next to your used tea bags.

HOW TO PLAN
AN IMPROMPTU TRIP

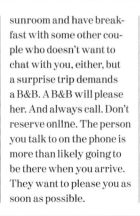

❶ ON THURSDAY AFTERNOON, check the weather. If it's going to be a nice weekend in your general vicinity, proceed.

❷ PICK A PLACE somewhere between two and three hours away, so you can leave work early, pick her up, and be there by eight.

❸ BOOK A B&B. Of course you don't want to sit in a sunroom and have breakfast with some other couple who doesn't want to chat with you, either, but a surprise trip demands a B&B. A B&B will please her. And always call. Don't reserve online. The person you talk to on the phone is more than likely going to be there when you arrive. They want to please you as soon as possible.

❹ CALL HER UP and say: "Let's get away. You deserve it." Establish that this trip is a gift. But a modest one.

❺ LOWER EXPECTATIONS. On the way there, say things like "You know, it's not a fancy hotel or anything." Or "It's probably going to be dead in Mystic this time of year." The worse you set it up, the more magical the weekend.

THE SICK NEST

WHEN A WOMAN FALLS ILL, SHE NEEDS YOU TO CREATE
AN ENVIRONMENT FOR HER CONVALESCENCE—A SICK NEST.
SHE WILL NOTICE, AND SHE WILL REMEMBER.

THE CHECKLIST

☐ **Water.**
With a straw.

☐ **Sofa** in front of the TV, padded
with every blanket and pillow you
can find.

☐ **Stack of movies.** Keep in mind that
sick people have lower cinematic
standards.

☐ **Remote controls** within reach.

☐ **Tissues.** The kind with lotion or
aloe in them, and a small trash can
to toss them in.

☐ **Herbal teas.** Four boxes of
assorted varieties.

☐ **Magazines.**

☐ **Her phone charger,** rigged up with
an extension cord if necessary.

☐ **Saltines,** the universal illness
cracker.

☐ **Ginger ale,** the universal illness
drink.

☐ **The window,** opened periodically.

☐ **Washcloth,** offered every once
in a while. (Hot or cold, as she
wishes.) Makes her feel clean,
which every woman enjoys.

☐ **Ibuprofen** or acetaminophen as
required.

☐ **Breakfast-in-bed tray.** To put all
this stuff on.

NOTES ON
WORRY-FREE
OGLING

NO SUNGLASSES?
HERE'S HOW TO APPRECIATE
A BEAUTIFUL WOMAN
AND GET AWAY WITH IT.

HOW TO AVOID GETTING CAUGHT

Position yourself so that the person you wish to ogle is between you and something you're actually allowed to look at (e.g., the ocean at the beach, or the television at a bar). Do it alone. By yourself, it's a discreet act of appreciation, like watching a sunset. When done with a couple other guys, however, you draw attention to yourselves, and what was harmless can seem predatory and disrespectful.

**YOU'VE BEEN CAUGHT.
WHAT NOW?**

Shift your attention immediately to the object in the background and hope she understands you weren't actually looking at her. *Or...*

... If she doesn't buy that, approach her and say, "Excuse me, but is your name [insert name here] and did you go to [insert name of your alma mater here]?" When she says no, apologize and say she reminded you of an old friend from college. Walk away and don't so much as breathe in her direction again. *Or...*

... Be bold. Maintain eye contact and smile, because if you act like what you did was wrong, then she's more inclined to think it was wrong. If you had any interest beyond ogling, go say hello. And, if applicable, remove wedding band.

HOW TO

BUY LINGERIE

❶ Figure out her size. Do this before you get to the store. Check her closet, or even the bra she left on the floor when she went in for a shower. And then be smart. For anything related to her breasts, err on the side of too big. For her ass, go small. Even if she has to return it, she'll be flattered. Keep in mind that higher-cut panties flatter shorter or thicker women by elongating legs. Boy shorts are hot on taller women or those who aren't so hoppy. If you want to be extra safe, get something with a less specific size (small, medium, large), like a black lace robe or negligee.

❷ Figure out your store. All women love La Perla, but that can be a little pricey, so try its Malizia line. It's just as nice, less expensive, and— most important—still says La Perla on the tag. Agent Provocateur is a good option if you want something more fantasy-related. And Victoria's Secret always works. It has a regular line, which is really affordable and well made, and also its Pink label, in case you want to see her in something more sweet and innocent.

❸ Pick a genre. If kinky, try lace in black or red. For sweet, stick with cotton in pink, baby blue, or white. If you want something that'll make her hate you, try plaid or polka dot.

❹ Remember comfort. Whereas most men want lingerie to come off as quickly as possible, women enjoy wearing it longer. They feel sexy in it, even if it's under their clothes.

❺ Ask questions. Frank questions. Don't worry, the salespeople have heard worse. They're there to help.

❻ Pay.

FOUR WAYS OF THE PANTY

WHAT SHE'S TELLING YOU WITH HER UNDERWEAR

BRIEFS

I've got a million things to do today, and I'm not in the mood.

BOYSHORTS

I'm looking to have some fun.

THONG

Don't get too excited. I'm only wearing this so I don't have a visible panty line, okay?

G-STRING

My name is Fantasia. Need a date?

HOW TO
ROCK THE MAN
IN THE BOAT

IMAGINE THAT YOU are a cake decorator with a range of fancy nibs to affix to the tip of your pastry bag. You can pipe rosettes and leaves all day, but no one needs that much sugar. The theatrical flourishes and jabs you've learned from your trusty porn are like that: the frosting on the frosting. A good pastry chef uses his nibs sparingly and aims

foremost for a thick, smooth application. Simply imagine the tool you'd need for such a job (no, it's not a knife, mallet, meat thermometer, or tongs, and certainly not a turkey baster) and try to mimic its shape and action with your tongue, fingers, or sleek Japanese device. Go slowly, be sedulous and heedful, and don't stop until the cake is done.

HOW TO READ HER FACE

A VISUAL GUIDE

| Highly controlled anger | Disgust | A mix of anger and enjoyment |
| Polite smile | Concentration | Pleasure |

WITH THANKS TO PAUL EKMAN, CREATOR THE FACIAL ACTION CODING SYSTEM
AND AUTHOR OF EMOTIONS REVEALED.

HOW TO CONSOLE A CRYING WOMAN

❶ Keep a handkerchief on your person. A clean one, since it's not for you. It's for the crying woman.

❷ When you encounter the crying woman (and she needs to be sobbing as if she's been hurt—never approach a woman who is merely weeping or teary), approach her as if you're advancing on a wounded animal that might still be able to bite—slowly, thoughtfully. Pull out the handkerchief.

❸ Say: "I'm sorry to disturb you, but is there anything I can do to help?"

❹ Whether she responds or not, offer the still-folded handkerchief. Point out that it's clean. This should make her laugh.

❺ If she hasn't yet told you to go away (and if she tells you to go away, do so immediately), ask what you might specifically be able to do: stay with her, call the police, listen to her problems, tap dance.

❻ Proceed according to her wishes until she says she's fine. Tell her to keep the hanky.

HOW MUCH IS TOO MUCH?

THE SEXUAL SUGGESTIONS OF A BOLD MAN

PROSECCO
-
CHOCOLATE-DIPPED FRUIT
-
ROSE PETALS
-
SCENTED OILS
-
MENTHOLATED RUBS
-
SALVIA
-
(BOUNDARY OF GOOD TASTE)
-
CLOTHESPINS
-
BRADS
-
SPECULUM
-
SOFT SWINGING
-
LIGHT ASPHYXIA
-
CATTLE BELLS
-
CATTLE PRODS
-
CATTLE

HOW TO **CALL IT OFF**

The ideal location is her home. There's no check to be paid, no coat to get from coat check. She can make a scene. Let her throw you out if she wants.

If she does throw you out, say, "I'm sorry" and calmly leave.

Be vague about your reasons, so as not to give the impression that there's one thing she can fix and everything will be okay. (Example: "It's a lot of things, things I've brought up in the past, but really it's just that I'm not focused on you like I should be, and that's not fair to you.") But not so vague that she has no idea why you're breaking up with her. Then you just come off as a dick.

You might feel tempted to say, "I really hope we can stay friends." Resist.

Bring a photo of the two of you. Show it to her. Tell her you're going to keep it, as a reminder of the fun you had. No reason not to end on a high note.

Do all of this at a time when you have nowhere else to be. Like, don't go over to break up with her if you want to be back in twenty minutes to see tip-off. She'll hear it in your voice.

Try not to have sex.

CAN IT BE SAVED?

· ·

A SPECIAL YOU-CALLED-HER-BY-THE-WRONG-NAME EDITION

THE PROBLEM	CAN IT BE SAVED?	THE SOLUTION
You can't remember her name, or you didn't catch it the first time around.	Yes.	Apologize and blame the noise level of the room in which you met.
You mispronounce her name.	Yes, provided it's a minute difference. For instance, if her name is Cara, it's okay to say *care-uh* instead of *car-uh*.	Admit that you had a friend in the past with a similarly spelled name.
You called her by your ex-girlfriend's name.	Yes, provided you do it only once.	Do not call her by your ex-girlfriend's name.

A GARDEN OF WHISPERS

I love you. ♥ I want you. ♥ You're the most beautiful woman in the world. ♥ In our haste to get to the bedroom, I think I left the oven on. Can you go check? ♥ You're mine and only mine. ♥ What? ♥ I just meant that no one else can have you. ♥ What? ♥ Anyway, I love you, and you're the most beautiful woman in the world.

THE APPROPRIATELY EMOTIVE

MAN'S GUIDE TO VALENTINE'S DAY

NEW RELATIONSHIP

MORNING GREETING "Happy Valentine's day!"

BREAKFAST In bed. Suggestion: Warm a large plate in the microwave for 15 seconds. Place one of the following (depending on her taste) on the warm plate: chocolate croissant; Boston cream from Dunkin' Donuts; plain bagel, toasted, with melted butter and some good sea salt on top.

4:00 P.M. TEXT "Your day is only going to get better."

DINNER OUT

GO SEE A NEW MOVIE

DRAW A BUBBLE BATH Throw a bottle containing a romantic message into the bath. Exclaim: "Oh, look what the tide brought in!"

STREW ROSE PETALS That indicates a route from bathroom to bedroom.

CLOSING REMARKS "Should we take this to the bedroom?"

LONG-TERM RELATIONSHIP

MORNING GREETING "Happy Valentine's Day."

BREAKFAST At the table like civilized people. Because breakfast in bed is a misguided notion (crumbs, etc.). See above for suggestions. Also, a single flower in a small vase.

4:00 P.M. TEXT "Can you pick up the champagne?"

DINNER IN

WATCH SUGGESTED FILM *City Lights*, Charlie Chaplin's touching, funny story about a tramp in love with a blind flower girl.

FREE TIME Catch up on e-mails, update Tumblr account, improvise displays of affection, etc.

CLOSING REMARKS "Let's take this to the bedroom. Or if you're sleepy, we can pick this up on Saturday."

ALONE

MORNING GREETING "Hello, Tuesday!"

BREAKFAST Divide previous suggestion in half.

FREE TIME Catch up on e-mails, update Tumblr account, improvise displays of affection, etc.

CLOSING REMARKS "Hello, RedTube!"

THE BEST-MADE BED

NOTE: USE ONLY CRISP, FLAT SHEETS PROCESSED WITH LIGHT STARCH AND SOFTENER FOR THE PROPER EMOTIONAL EXPERIENCE. NO FITTED SHEETS.

❶ WITH YOUR FIRST SHEET, cover the top of the mattress from left to right and top to bottom. Tuck the edges of the sheet underneath the bed while creating boxed corners (i.e., tight tucks). This is the only sheet you will tuck.

❷ COVER THE FIRST SHEET with a second sheet, and then fold the top half of the second sheet over the bottom half so that the foot of the bed is the only part covered with the second sheet. This is called the foot fold, and it is good.

❸ PLACE A FEATHERED DUVET on top of the first and second sheets. This will serve as simply a coverlet.

❹ TAKE YOUR TOP SHEET and lay it over the comforter and the other two sheets; fold both the comforter and the top sheet from the top down a foot away from the headboard.

❺ ADORN THE TOP of the bed with feather pillows. Stare in amazement.

❻ FIND A WOMAN who can help you mess it up.

CHAPTER FOUR

ON WEDDINGS

WHAT I'VE LEARNED

I got married because I wanted to do something that was more than I understood, because my feelings were more than I understood.
—MANDY PATINKIN

There's no secret to a successful marriage. I love my wife. More important than that, I really like her.
—STING

THE RULES

RULE NO. 1,006:
There is never a reason a couple should share one e-mail account.

RULE NO. 1,017:
If it bends, it's funny. If it bends two ways, it's even funnier. If it bends three ways, marry it.

RULE NO. 1,023:
After your fifth divorce, you gotta start wondering if maybe it's you.

FREQUENTLY ASKED

-QUESTIONS-

HOW TO GO OFF REGISTRY

Q.	A.
Should I bring my gift to the wedding?	No. Ship it to the newlyweds at home.
May I bring my kids?	Are those kids the flower girl or ring bearer? If not, then no.
May I take my coat off to dance?	Yes, but only after the groom or his father does so.
Is there a fool-proof way to avoid a hangover?	No. Just take a few Advil before bed, and realize you aren't alone.
When may I leave?	When the dinner is concluded and the cake has been cut.
But I'm the groom.	In that case, not until the last light is turned off.
Should I tip the bartender?	Can't hurt. You know how annoying you people can be.
You people?	That joke's a little old by now, don't you think?

STEP ONE

ATM

SEATING: A HOW-TO

BEHAVIORAL TIPS FOR OPTIMIZING YOUR RECEPTION-TABLE FUN

- Never try to change your table assignment. You know better than that.

- If only a few places at the table have been taken, don't sit as far away from them as possible. Make a new friend.

- Similarly, don't leave just one spot between you and another guest. Most people are here with a date.

- Introduce yourself as people sit. It's easier to remember names for a few small groups than for one large one.

- No asking for seconds. Even if it was delicious. (But you can probably sneak another piece of cake.)

- Stop clinking your glass. It's strange to enjoy watching other people kiss that much.

- It is perfectly acceptable to continue eating during the toast(s).

- Talking, however, should be saved until the toasts are finished. Even if you all agree the toasts are boring.

- Limit your alcohol consumption. (This will also help with the tip above.)

THE WORST-CASE-SCENARIO GUIDE TO

BEING A GOOD GROOMSMAN

THREE PROBLEMATIC SCENARIOS, THREE HEROIC SOLUTIONS

ISSUE: With all heads turned up the aisle toward the bride, no one sees Grandma struggling to get out of her chair.

RESPONSIBILITY: Help her. You can't be blamed for ostentatious chivalry, since no one's looking at you anyway. When she's stable (and before the bride—and the group gaze—reaches you), return to your place in the wedding party.

ISSUE: No one's dancing.

RESPONSIBILITY: Grab a (willing) mom, grandma, or child and lead her to the dance floor. (Not your date. That's not as fun or cute to watch.) People will soon follow your lead. If for whatever reason they don't, give up when the song is over. Longer than that and you risk coming off as creepy.

ISSUE: Cousin Tina isn't having much fun.

RESPONSIBILITY: Get her a drink. Ask her to tell you an embarrassing story about the bride/groom. Try to get her to dance or to watch you do so. Giving her something to focus on will make her feel less uncomfortable. But remember: you owe her 20 minutes, tops. If she's still bored at that point, she'll be that way all night.

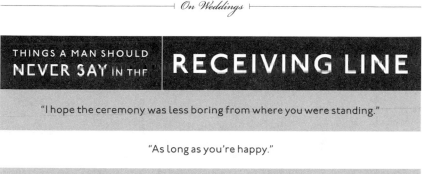

THINGS A MAN SHOULD NEVER SAY IN THE RECEIVING LINE

"I hope the ceremony was less boring from where you were standing."

"As long as you're happy."

"Once a cheater, always a cheater."

"Tell me how you guys met."

"Second times a charm. Here's hoping, at least."

"I called dibs. It's a real thing."

"Is THAT the easy one?"

"You must have heard of it, P-R-I-M-A...N-O-C..."

"Spoiler alert! I got you the 12-piece porcelain tea set!"

"Hmpf. Sure. White."

SO YOU MET **SOMEONE**

THEIR RELATION TO THE BRIDE OR GROOM

YOUR RELATION TO THE BRIDE OR GROOM

	FRIEND	CLOSE FRIEND	RELATIVE
FRIEND	proceed	proceed	⚠
CLOSE FRIEND	proceed	⚠	⚠
RELATIVE	proceed	proceed	✗
DISTANT RELATIVE	proceed	proceed	✗
COWORKER	proceed	⚠	⚠
GUEST'S DATE	proceed	proceed	proceed
BRIDE	✗	✗	✗
GROOM	✗	✗	✗

LEGEND ➤ *PROCEED*

CAN YOU ACT ON YOUR NEW FEELINGS? DEPENDS.

THEIR RELATION TO THE BRIDE OR GROOM

DISTANT RELATIVE	COWORKER	GUEST'S DATE	BRIDE	GROOM
🙌	⚠️	🙌	X	X
⚠️	⚠️	⚠️	X	X
X	🙌	🙌	X	X
⚠️	🙌	🙌	X	X
🙌	⚠️	🙌	X	X
🙌	🙌	🙌	X	X
X	X	X		🙌
X	X	X	🙌	

(right margin, vertical) YOUR RELATION TO THE BRIDE OR GROOM

⚠️ PROCEED WITH CAUTION X UNADVISED

LORD OF THE DANCE

A FEW RULES FOR CUTTING A RESPECTABLE RUG

Always lead your date to the dance floor. It's a little formal, but so are weddings.

No dipping.

Spins, however, are encouraged. (Just remember that she's been drinking.)

If you know the mother of the bride or groom, ask her for a dance. It's her day, too.

Was that air drumming? Carry on.

If your efforts to start a group rendition of the Electric Slide do not find immediate group approval, move on.

Are you the only one tangoing? Stop.

Have another drink.

Relax.

Stop worrying about how you'll look in pictures.

SO YOU WANT TO BUY A DIAMOND

What we talk about when we talk about proposing

COLOR

There are pink and yellow and even black diamonds, but she probably wants a white one. The whiter the stone, the higher the price, with the official grade range running from D (colorless) to Z (a light yellow). Anything higher than an I (i.e., D to H) will appear white enough for the most discerning eyes.

CUT

You've got plenty of options, and keep in mind that the deeper the stone, the more light it will reflect and the more sparkle it will give off. Here are a few popular cuts:

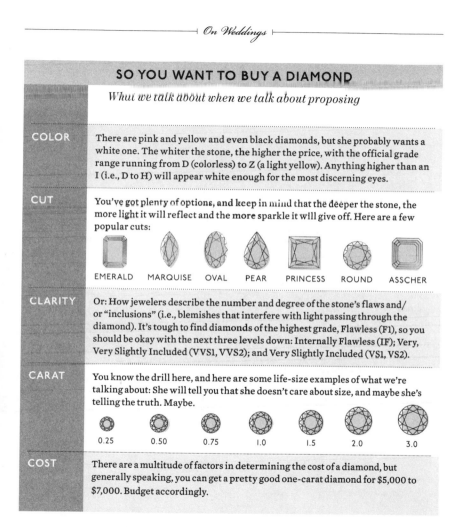

EMERALD MARQUISE OVAL PEAR PRINCESS ROUND ASSCHER

CLARITY

Or: How jewelers describe the number and degree of the stone's flaws and/or "inclusions" (i.e., blemishes that interfere with light passing through the diamond). It's tough to find diamonds of the highest grade, Flawless (Fl), so you should be okay with the next three levels down: Internally Flawless (IF); Very, Very Slightly Included (VVS1, VVS2); and Very Slightly Included (VS1, VS2).

CARAT

You know the drill here, and here are some life-size examples of what we're talking about: She will tell you that she doesn't care about size, and maybe she's telling the truth. Maybe.

0.25   0.50   0.75   1.0   1.5   2.0   3.0

COST

There are a multitude of factors in determining the cost of a diamond, but generally speaking, you can get a pretty good one-carat diamond for $5,000 to $7,000. Budget accordingly.

HOW TO **NAVIGATE THE AFTERPARTY**

THE WEDDING IS OVER. THE FUN, NOT SO MUCH

➤ The bride and groom may change clothes. You should not. Taking a break between the wedding and afterparty means getting a chance to sit down. Which means a chance to fall asleep. Don't preempt your second wind.

➤ With a thinned-out crowd, the bride and groom **[A]** no longer have responsibilities— or an obligation to talk to distant relatives. This is your best chance to spend some time with them.

➤ Make sure you have cash. Cash bar at the reception is annoying. Cash bar at the afterparty is standard.

➤ Stick with beer **[B]**. You're winding down at this point, for one thing, and it's easier to buy rounds without taking orders.

➤ Most events will provide some sort of comfort food, but if not, you don't want to be the only person sitting down to a greasy bag of delivery. Get a few people together and order a bunch of pizzas **[C]** for the room. Remember; you're not the only one who's drunk and hungry. You'll be a hero.

➤ If that lonely bridesmaid **[D]** is going to make her move, now is the time. Avoid/engage accordingly.

➤ If there's a TV **[E]**, it will be surrounded by older men. They don't want to talk. But they'd love for you to join them.

➤ Everyone's had a bit to drink, which makes it your best time to meet new people. Just don't stay too long with one group and wear out your welcome.

➤ Unlike at the reception, you don't have to stay to a certain point. Stay until the room starts spinning or the bride's cousin corners you to discuss his thoughts on health care.

➤ If your sweet-talking skills are still functional, try to get the bartender **[F]** to give you a leftover bottle of booze. Somebody's gotta start the after-afterparty, right?

THE REASONABLY ENTHUSIASTIC

GROOM'S TO-DO LIST

BECAUSE SHE'S NOT THE ONLY ONE
WITH RESPONSIBILITIES

☐ PROPOSE.

☐ SUBMIT engagement announcement to the local paper, town gossip, or AOL Patch blogger.

☐ CHOOSE your best man (see page 64 for help) and groomsmen.

☐ DETERMINE budget. Add 20 percent.

☐ BUILD a guest list. (Matrimony tip: The more weddings you've had, the fewer people you invite.)

☐ BOOK venue, officiant, music, photographer, florist, wedding planner, caterer, hotel block, invitation designer, rehearsal dinner location, honeymoon, et cet.

☐ DON'T let her know that you referred to anything as "et cet."

☐ OBTAIN marriage license.

☐ BUY rings.

☐ SELECT gifts for your groomsmen.

☐ ESTABLISH reception hashtag (for the Instagramming!)

☐ PANIC. Briefly.

☐ SHOW up.

☐ SMILE.

☐ EAT.

☐ DANCE a bit.

☐ SMILE.

☐ SLEEP.

☐ BRUNCH.

☐ HONEYMOON.

A FEW WORDS FOR A MAN ON HIS WEDDING DAY

THE WORST THING that can happen at the ceremony will not happen. You will not faint. You will not flub your lines. The best man will not throw up. She will not run away from you and get on a bus. No uncle will split his suit pants bending over. Nothing that America's Funniest Home Videos leads you to believe may happen will happen. Because unless you've been practicing an elaborate entrance involving choreography and the bride's being carried in on a litter (which is a mistake, frankly, but you will get through it), this is not a high-pressure situation. Almost everything is scripted, prescribed, watched over, ordained by God, and decreed by the state. And everyone knows what their role is— you, your bride, the officiant, the guests, the bored waiters, everyone.

Also, you have your shit together. This is not a small thing. She has her shit together, too. And the people around you have their shit together. That's why you're all gathered on this glorious day: to celebrate having your shit together.

You know what to expect at the ceremony. It's on the program. And it includes getting married. Not wanting to be married. Which is not simple. Nor being married. Which is not simple. But getting married. Which is simple. Walk and smile. Say "I do." Walk and smile. Done.

The reception is also simple—if you know how to attend a party, you know how to attend your own reception—but it's not quite as simple as the ceremony. Because it involves one thing that the both of you and the both of you alone must independently express without prompting: Thanks. Everyone must be thanked, Even that guy over there. This is a requirement. For efficiency's sake, do this when people are still seated at tables. As soon as the appetizer course is served, begin going around to each table (both of you) to offer thanks and bask in the good wishes. Pace yourself. Do a few tables, go eat something, do a few more tables, go drink something (not too much), do a few more tables, and you'll be done before dessert. When you've walked away from the last table, you will be seen as a grateful man. And she will be seen as lucky to have you. Easy. Congratulations.

A QUIZ

HOW TO CHOOSE YOUR BEST MAN

YOUR BEST FRIEND IS NOT ALWAYS YOUR BEST CHOICE.
HAND OUT TO ALL INTERESTED PARTIES.

1. Are you the brother of the groom?
a) Yes (100)
b) No (0)

2. Are you the father of the groom?
a) Yes (-50)
b) No (5)

c) Yes, but this is the South and it's tradition. (100)

3. Would friends characterize you as responsible?
a) Yes (10)
b) No (0)

4. Fun?
a) Yes (10)
b) No (0)

5. Selfish?
a) Yes (-5)
b) No (0)

6. If, for whatever reason, the groom is unable to perform his duties through this marriage, are you willing to step up?
a) Of course. (-10)
b) That's not real. (5)

7. Breath mint?
a) Sure, thanks. (0)
b) I always carry them. Here you go. (5)

8. Beer pong?
a) Where!? (5)
b) I'm an adult. (-10)

9. True or false: If no one is dancing, it is the best man's responsibility to get things started.
a) True (5)
b) False (0)
c) I assure you that there will never be a time when no one is dancing, drinking, hugging, or attempting all three simultaneously. (15)

10. What is your ideal bachelor party?
a) A weekend away with ten or so good

friends. Some
beers. Some
grilling. (10)

b) A strip club or
something. (0)

c) Movie night! (-5)

**11. Take 4 points off
your score for
each of the fol-
lowing words or
phrases you've
used in the past
six months.**

a) You da man!

b) Broseph.

c) Comme ci,
comme ca.

d) Dude. It's
a whole
new Hobbit
triology.

e) Cray cray.

f) I hate to bring
it up, but you
still owe me
two dollars.

**12. Can I trust you
to hold on to
the rings?**

a) Yes (5)

b) No (-5)

c) I'm offended
that you had
to ask. (10)

d) Trick question!
I'm not your
ring bearer (-5)

**13. My niece goes
missing at the
reception. What
do you do?**

a) Make sure no
one's accusing
me of losing
her (-10)

b) Mention it to
her parents.
(-5)

c) Check the
sofas and
closets; she
probably just
fell asleep. (5)

d) Bring her
back from the
dance floor,
apologize,
and let them
be surprised
when they
see that the
photographer
got one of
those cute
pictures in
which she's
dancing by
standing on
your shoes.
(10)

**14. Which of the
following sen-
tences are you
most likely
to use in your
toast?**

a) I love you guys.
(10)

b) If I can find
someone who
makes me
half as happy
as she makes
you, I'll con-
sider myself a
lucky man. (5)

c) You sure went
through a lot
of candidates
before settling
on this one.
(-10)

d) You sure went
through a lot
of candidates
before settling
for this one.
(-20)

e) She should be
with me. (-50)

**15. Can you be
appropriate in
front of older
people?**

a) Yes (10)

b) No (-10)

**16. My nana will be
there.**

a) Cute (5)

b) Let it go. I
apologized.
(-15)

**17. We need a ride
to the airport,
please.**

a) Gladly. Let me
get my keys. (5)

b) Me, too. (-5)

-ANSWER KEY-

• **MORE THAN 100
TOTAL POINTS**
You will be the
best man.

• **50 TO 100 POINTS**
You'll probably
be a groomsman.
That's still
something.

• **FEWER THAN
50 POINTS**
Consider your-
self lucky to be
invited.

THE ART OF
TOASTING

by Don Rickles

Prepare nothing and be confident. I have no idea what I'm going to say when I stand up to give a toast. But I do know that anything I say I find funny. If you start questioning your toast, you're in a lot of trouble. So find the right attitude and go with it. Riff on the bride or groom for most of it. Just be sure to be respectful.

Be sure not to say something sappy in the middle of the toast. You put kindness in the middle and everybody will leave. Do kindness at the end. I call it my rabbi speech. It's where you let the couple know that you really care about them. That's why you're there. Because you shouldn't be toasting someone you don't like.

THE ART OF BEING TOASTED

Try to keep a low profile. Don't talk to one group of people for too long—less chance of saying something stupid. Drink water. Smile. Not that much. Oh, you meant that way? Just sit and smile.

WEDDING PREP

—

One of these vows is not like the others. Find it.

To HAVE
....

To HOLD
....

To LOVE
....

To CHERISH
....

To LISTEN TO
....

To VALUE
....

To RESPECT
....

To HONOR
....

To MONITOR
CLOSELY
at all times
....

YOUR WEDDING PHOTO

························

IT'S THE MOST LASTING PICTURE YOU'LL EVER TAKE.
MAKE IT GOOD.

Never look at the camera.

♥

Avoid the setup. A candid shot captures real emotion, from body language to hand placement.

♥

Don't be afraid of the dress. You just married this woman, right? If you're leaning in to avoid damaging her dress, you'll leave a gap between you, which doesn't exactly convey love.

♥

If you're wearing a jacket, try not to raise your arms, unless you want to look like you're wearing a cape.

The kiss shot: Make sure both hands are on the bride. A lot of grooms leave one arm hanging in front. Strange. Not flattering.

♥

Put one foot slightly behind the other, directly beneath your spine. It forces you to stand up straight.

♥

Have the photographer get on a stool. The slight downward angle and a telephoto lens flatten features and generally make everyone look more beautiful.

♥

No mustaches.

WITH THIS RING (OR MAYBE THAT ONE)

··

A BRIEF BUT ILLUMINATING LOOK AT WEDDING BANDS.

STYLES

DOMED — The classic choice. Simple and understated. Because they are peaked (when looked at in profile), domed rings can be slightly more susceptible to dings.

PATTERNED — Popular options are milgrain (textured along the edges), woven (a simple over-under pattern), and wave (you know, the ocean).

FLAT — As simple and under-stated as a domed ring, but with a level surface and squared edges for a modern feel.

GEMSTONE — When patterned rings just don't provide enough flash. The safest choice is diamonds, and only just a few. Try to keep them small.

METALS

GOLD is the most traditional. It was also the most popular until a few years ago, when sterling silver took over.

STERLING SILVER is a less expensive choice yet still has a high shine. It smudges easily, so be ready for frequent polishing.

PLATINUM is the most expensive option. But also the shiniest! (And thus the worst at hiding scratches.) Its hypoallergenic, too, which can be beneficial for up to 15 percent of men.

Your other two budget-friendly options are **TITANIUM**—hypoallergenic, light, and durable, with a matte finish—and **TUNGSTEN**, which is as shiny as silver but darker and more resistant to scratches.

CHAPTER FIVE

ON MONEY

WHAT I'VE LEARNED

My father gave me a two-dollar bill for my grade school graduation and said, "Hold on to this, and you'll never be broke." I still have it. A lot of times, that's all I've had. But I've never been broke.
—JOHN WOODEN

You have to fight for the last penny. If you don't fight for the last penny, you might lose the last ten million.
—SUMNER REDSTONE

THE RULES

RULE NO. 313:
After dinner, when you reach into your wallet a little more slowly than everyone else, trust us, they all notice.

RULE NO. 389:
No matter how poor you are, putting your pennies in rolls is, economically speaking, a waste of time.

RULE NO. 391:
You don't pay cash at the dentist.

— ESQUIRE PRESENTS —

YOUR FINANCIAL BIOGRAPHY

How to Earn, Save, and Spend at Every Age

<table>
<tr><td>AGE

25</td><td>AGE

35</td></tr>
<tr><td>

Status: Single. No kids. No mortgage. Making money.

Biggest expenses: Rent, cable, clothes, attending weddings, football pool, *Esquire* subscription, sandwiches.

Fears: None.

....

• At every age, you should have six months' expenses in liquid savings. For emergencies. But no one does that at twenty-five. Just start parking a few bucks each month in an online savings account.

• If you have a 401(k) and your employer matches contributions, pay in at least enough to take advantage of that.

• Get aggressive. Rule of thumb: you can put 70 percent of your money in stocks in your twenties, provided you've got the nuts to ride it out if the markets take a dive (and they will).

</td><td>

Status: Married. Two young kids. Solid job.

Biggest expenses: Mortgage or rent, groceries, football pool, the black hole into which you throw money to raise your children.

Fears: Affording college, not getting squat from Social Security someday, missing the next bubble, another huge collapse.

....

• Retirement trumps saving for college every time, so keep the 401(k) cooking. Your retirement savings are still collapse-proof.

• Reconcile the demands on your money with a Roth IRA. After five years you can take penalty-free distributions for qualified expenses, including your first home.

• Open a 529 plan for the kids' college. Compare plans at savingforcollege.com

</td></tr>
</table>

AGE 50

Status: Could use some retirement catch-up. Good career, but you never know.

Biggest expenses: Mortgage, home upkeep, property taxes, entertainment, kids' tuition.

Fears: Retirement, home value, America's diminishing role in the global economy.

• *Use a retirement work sheet to set goals—this one is good: choosetosave. org/ballpark. It asks stuff like when you think you'll die, but just go with it.*

• *Be less aggressive—50 percent stocks. But take enough risk to beat inflation. One way to do that is to buy gold (in an ETF, rather than owning coins).*

• *Consider an international fund.*

• *Make an extra mortgage payment each year. The less debt you have now, the better.*

AGE 72

Status: Retired. Could use some more income.

Biggest expenses: Greens fees? Sir, can you help us out? What are your biggest expenses?

Fear: Outliving your retirement savings.

• *Work a part-time job that you enjoy. Could be fun, and it—along with Social Security—will allow you to draw less from your retirement accounts, meaning your balances will stay invested longer and grow more. And if your investments bounce back, you can quit the hardware-store gig and go sailing.*

THE GLOSSARY
ABRIDGED

Baltic Dry Index: *Tracks the cost of shipping bulk basics like steel and concrete. Underrated economic indicator.*

Euro: *Newly favored reserve currency (formerly known as the dollar).*

Federal debt: *What the government owes its lenders—essentially, buyers of Treasuries. Major holders include China, Brazil, and your grandparents.*

Federal deficit: *The difference between revenue and spending—made up by selling bonds.*

50 Cent: *Rapper.*

Friedman, Milton: *Founder of postmodern macroeconomics, advocate of monetarism. See also: Republican.*

Keynes, John Maynard: *Founder of modern macroeconomics, advocate of government interventionism. See also: Democrat.*

Marx, Karl: *Founder of socialist economics, advocate of proletarian revolution. See also: dreamer.*

PE ration: *Price-per-share versus earnings-per-share of a publicly traded company. North of 50 to 1 is a little crazy.*

Smith, Adam: *Founder of classical economics, advocate of the theory of the invisible hand. See also: libertarian.*

Stagflation: *Something from the '70s.*

Voodoo economics: *Reagan policy claiming that cutting taxes would make everyone rich. Syn: supply-side economics.*

White swan: *An event so obvious that the market ignores it. Like, say, a housing bubble.*

THE 20 IMMUTABLE LAWS OF

PERSONAL FINANCE

by Ken Kurson

I. **NEVER PAY CASH FOR A CAR**. Not while interest rates are zero to 1 percent.

2. **NEVER CATCH A FALLING KNIFE**. Or, You're less knowledgeable than whoever sits on the opposite side of all investments. The only thing that can save you is your knowledge of that fact. Two guys are watching a roulette wheel. Red comes up four times in a row. The first guy concludes, "Red is hot. I'm putting it all on red." The second guy says, "Black is due. I'm putting it all on black." The fair end to this story would be the wheel landing on 0 or 00, so they both lose. In real life, the ending is equally grim: Both guys shuffle their chips around, making opposite bets until the casino's 5.26 percent advantage leaves them both poorer. In real life, that house edge is a commission or a transaction cost or a fee that eats away your principal (and your "winnings") in identical fashion. If something is a good idea, it is not because of what happened in the past. It is because

you are making an informed bet on what is going to happen. Apple provides a perfect example. Is it now a great investment because it has fallen so much? Or is it smart to sell because the market hates it? The smartest analysis is what you think Apple is worth based on its price right now. All investing is price versus value. Yesterday's price and value count for zero.

3. DIVERSIFY YOUR INVESTMENTS.

This is not to improve your results. In fact, if you do find that once-in-a-lifetime long shot that comes in, diversification will prevent you from taking full advantage. But diversification reminds you that it's usually fruitless to spend the energy trying to outperform professionals at their game. Consequently...

4. YOUR BEST INVESTMENT IS IN A BROAD BASKET OF U.S. EQUITIES.

The '00s were brutal on U. S. stock markets—1.41 percent over ten years. But even including the worst collapse in both equity prices and the very markets themselves that occurred in 2007 and 2008, it's not even close. The last thirty years, from the beginning of the '80s through the end of 2010, the compound annualized return of the S&P 500 was 10.71 percent. Last twenty years, it was 9.14 percent. Last forty years, it was 10.14 percent. And it's my personal

belief that the teens are going to be (continue to be, actually) a great decade for U.S. equities. With government policies that encourage—practically command—cash hoarding, and even the biggest innovators in the country forced to pay giant dividends or stoke the share price with buybacks, there's really nowhere else to go. The best investment an American can make when factoring both returns and quality of life (i.e., not trying to outperform professionals while paying ludicrous trading fees) is a low-cost, highly rated index fund of American equities.

5. BUT YOUR REAL BEST INVESTMENT—DEFINITELY IN TIME, POSSIBLY IN MONEY—IS IN YOURSELF. You are a sucker in most investment markets. Unless you become a professional, you're an underdog to outperform them. Apply most of your time, effort, and money to your business or career, where you are the professional and the favorite.

6. SAVE FOR RETIREMENT. We've grown obsessed with a concept introduced by Morningstar as it moves into the money-management business. You've probably heard of the investing concepts "alpha" and "beta," which are used to measure the riskiness of your portfolio and its performance variance from a like basket of investments.

Suddenly, in 2012, there's gamma, which measures the benefits that can be taken simply by planning smartly. The results are unbelievable—as much as 28.8 percent in additional retirement income by observing optimal curves for five areas: asset allocation, withdrawal, annuities, tax efficiency, and liability protection. It is amazing to me that the most considered field of investing can still yield surprising results, but I've been studying the concept and its effects, and they're real. There's not space to go into it here, but consider every American you know who's over sixty. The ones who saved enough and prepared for retirement are going to live longer and more happily than the ones who did not.

7. BUT NOT UNTIL YOU'VE PAID OFF YOUR CREDIT CARD. Half of Americans carry a credit-card balance, and they're paying roughly 14 percent on it. Startlingly, a lot of that 50 percent are also saving for retirement, including many who stock their 401(k) or IRA money in fixed-income funds that are doing 5 percent. According to Morningstar, a guy who pays off his credit-card balance and then invests for retirement will increase his 401(k) at retirement by 14.1 percent. The math changes here when considering retirement plans that include "free money" from an employer in the form of a 401(k) match,

which brings about a sub rule: Always take free money, even when it hurts to do so.

8. DON'T GET DIVORCED. Same: Don't have kids to save your marriage. Don't buy a house to save your marriage.

9. GET A HOUSE. The interest is tax deductible, and for a thirty-year mortgage, most of your initial payments are interest. It could be a good investment if you choose wisely. And you can live in it and have your life more positively influenced by it than by any other possession.

10. INSURE ONLY AGAINST DEVAS-TATING EVENTUALITIES. Insurance is a hedge against a catastrophic event. Don't insure against minor expenses or expenses that might be sad and hard to think about but won't bankrupt you. Insurance means taking the other side of the bet with someone who knows the odds better than you and profits only to the extent of your ignorance. The only reasons to get insurance are a) if you are smarter than the people against whom you are betting, or b) if you can afford to pay a marginal cost against a catastrophic event, cost, or outcome. Health insurance, term life insurance (whole or universal life is for suckers only), car insurance (only to the degree you need it by law and to which you need to protect your assets against catastrophe), homeowners insurance, flood insurance—those are the products you should consider. I go nuts when I see ads (mostly on Judge Joe Brown) for funeral insurance or (on The Price Is Right) for insurance against the death of a child or grandchild. Extended warranties, identity-theft protection, flight insurance at the airport? Please. Buy what you need for the reason you need it. Don't buy life insurance as an investment, unless you'd pay more for an oil change if the mechanic promised to invest the difference.

II. TRANSACTION AND CARRYING COSTS.

Find and avoid them unless you have no choice or you can make a reasoned assessment of what you are getting for your money. Many "great" investments could turn out to be not so great once you factor in transaction costs: frequent stock trading, real estate.

12. WHAT YOU SPEND IS AS IMPORTANT AS WHAT YOU MAKE.

How much do you spend on vacations? Cars? Hobbies? Restaurants? Vices? I believe in spending. I don't want to count every nickel. And I've always believed that I can make more money—that's one ninth of the reason I'm writing this article. But taxes make it an uneven proposition—understand that if you are falling short by, say, $5,000 a year, you have only two choices: Spend $5,000 less. Or, depending on your tax bracket, earn about $6,500 more.

13. PAY UNTO CAESAR, BUT NOT A PENNY MORE.

Tax avoidance usually ends badly. First, you likely have increased costs for accounting and legal advice. Second, at a minimum you have the cost of the stress while you sweat out long, loophole-filled statutes of limitations. (Remember, the same people imposing those taxes are the ones who decide the length of the statute of limitations.) Third, directing your fortune building through tax avoidance can seriously limit your investment options and color your judgment. Two extremes to avoid: Elvis

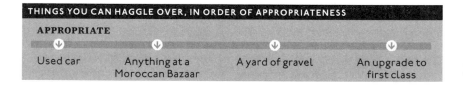

THINGS YOU CAN HAGGLE OVER, IN ORDER OF APPROPRIATENESS

APPROPRIATE

| Used car | Anything at a Moroccan Bazaar | A yard of gravel | An upgrade to first class |

Presley, who always paid the top tax rate when it was over 70 percent (Hell, I'll just make more money if I need more.) The other is a professional gambling friend who was so tax-averse that most of his investments ended up being with scam artists. They promised him no paper trail, no K-1's or 1099's or W-2's, and all his (nonexistent) returns in untraceable cash.

14. BE CAREFUL WHOM YOU PAY FOR ADVICE—ESPECIALLY IF THEY CLAIM IT'S FREE. Commission can be a conflict of interest. Your first mistake when selling a house is agreeing on a listing price with the real estate agent. The agent gets a commission on the sale, but if he convinces you to sell for, say, 85 percent of full price, he'll get 85 percent of his commission and have a super easy selling job because you're giving your house away. Likewise, in the offer-counteroffer process, his financial interest is in completing the deal and banking a commission, not prolonging the selling process for a tiny commission increase.

15. MAINTENANCE OFTEN COSTS MORE THAN PURCHASE. Avoid horses, boats, airplanes, wives, kids, co-ops, time-shares, and country clubs.

16. IF YOU'RE OUT ON A LIMB, MAKE SURE YOU'RE WAY OUT THERE. Don't take a risk if you're going to be too quick to give up or cash in.

17. TAKE RISKS Take the biggest risks when you're young. But you're young for a long time. Because you take care of your body and seek joy in life, place your faith in something bigger than yourself.

18. BE ORGANIZED. If you want to know what it's like to deal with a loan shark, carry a $100 credit-card balance for two months. You'll not only pay 25 percent annual interest on that balance, but they'll hit you with a pair of $25 late fees. Your $100 debt is now $154 (300 percent annualized interest!), not including future increased lending rates. (Home-equity loan rates, for example, are based on credit

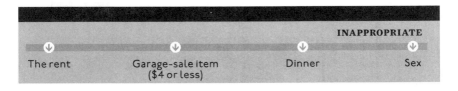

| The rent | Garage-sale item ($4 or less) | Dinner | **INAPPROPRIATE** Sex |

scores, so you'll pay more even on loans secured by your house once you mess up your credit.) Set up automatic bill payment based on credit-card due dates rather than arbitrary ones like "first of the month."

19. DISCOVER NEW THINGS WITH "PLAY MONEY."

It's hard to call this a rule because I think it speaks to my particular money psychology as a gambler, but I've found that my management skill is enhanced when I divide my mental wallet into real and play money. I observe all the rules above with the money my family and I depend on. But I've always set aside some dough for stuff that interests me and might result in a big score but won't devastate me if it goes to zero. My thing right now is Ripple, a bitcoin-related alternative currency, but it's ranged from speculative real estate investing to just plain gambling, some of which has actually turned a profit. The main value of this pressure-release valve is that it's kept me from dipping into my real money to chase some white horse.

20. USE FREEBIES.

Airlines build frequent-flier-mile costs into their prices, so you lose if you don't take maximum advantage. Same with credit-card points and customer-loyalty plans. But don't live your life as a quest to get the last dime out of your yogurt punch card.

— ESSENTIAL MONEY WISDOM —

Investment must be rational; if you don't understand it, don't do it.
—WARREN BUFFETT

Money doesn't talk, it swears.
—BOB DYLAN

For any sensible person, money is two things: a major liberating force and a great convenience. It's devastating to those who have in mind nothing else.
—JOHN KENNETH GALBRAITH

Money's only something you need in case you don't die tomorrow.
—CARL FOX, WALL STREET

Of all the icy blasts that blow on love, a request for money is the most chilling and havoc-wreaking.
—GUSTAVE FLAUBERT

CHAPTER SIX

ON TRAVEL

WHAT I'VE LEARNED

Flying private is the world's
greatest luxury.
You don't get jet-lagged.
—LARRY KING

I believe that all roads lead
to the same place—and that is
wherever all roads lead to.
—WILLIE NELSON

THE RULES

RULE NO. 515:
Cairo is the nicest city
with open sewers.

RULE NO. 578:
First class is to business class
is to coach as Groucho is to
Harpo is to Zeppo.

RULE NO. 591:
If you are a movie character in a hurry
and are driving through a rural area,
you will run into a herd of sheep
crossing the road.

TO WHEEL OR **NOT** TO WHEEL

What should you carry, what should you wheel,
and what should you leave for someone else?
A simple calculation.

$$X*(0.10†) + 10‡ = Y$$

* *Your weight.*

† *The American Chiropractic Association recommends carrying bags that weigh less than 10 percent of your body weight to avoid back strain.*

‡ *Because you are a man. Strong like ox.*

IF YOUR BAG WEIGHS LESS THAN Y, use a duffel.

IF YOUR BAG WEIGHS BETWEEN Y AND Y+10, get a wheeled bag. Anything more and you risk not being able to lift it into the overhead area. Shameful.

IF YOUR BAG WEIGHS MORE THAN Y+10, use a reasonably sized suitcase. And check it.

OR, A SIMPLER CALCULATION:

Can you carry it comfortably?
Then do. Anything more, wheel it.
Moving abroad, try a trunk.

THE PERFECTLY PACKED BAG

WHAT TO BRING IF YOU'RE TRAVELING FOR BUSINESS

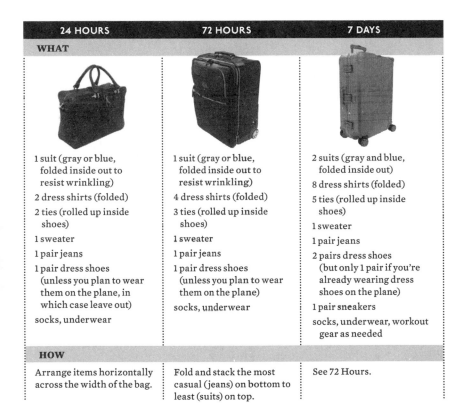

24 HOURS	72 HOURS	7 DAYS
WHAT		
1 suit (gray or blue, folded inside out to resist wrinkling)	1 suit (gray or blue, folded inside out to resist wrinkling)	2 suits (gray and blue, folded inside out)
2 dress shirts (folded)	4 dress shirts (folded)	8 dress shirts (folded)
2 ties (rolled up inside shoes)	3 ties (rolled up inside shoes)	5 ties (rolled up inside shoes)
1 sweater	1 sweater	1 sweater
1 pair jeans	1 pair jeans	1 pair jeans
1 pair dress shoes (unless you plan to wear them on the plane, in which case leave out)	1 pair dress shoes (unless you plan to wear them on the plane)	2 pairs dress shoes (but only 1 pair if you're already wearing dress shoes on the plane)
socks, underwear	socks, underwear	1 pair sneakers
		socks, underwear, workout gear as needed
HOW		
Arrange items horizontally across the width of the bag.	Fold and stack the most casual (jeans) on bottom to least (suits) on top.	See 72 Hours.

HOW TO
NAVIGATE THE AIRPORT BAR
....
BECAUSE A LAYOVER SHOULD NEVER END IN A HANGOVER

That frozen-margarita machine churning away on the back counter?
You may wonder about its contents, but never sample them.

■

You're ordering a beer, maybe a Scotch, neat.
Airport bartenders are not mixologists. They're barely bartenders.

■

If you are engaged in conversation, be cordial.
And brief. And subtle when you turn your gaze back to ESPN.

■

The bartender does not want to charge your phone for you,
even if you're "low on juice."

■

Your jacket goes on the back of your chair.
Your bag goes under it. Neither goes on the chair beside you.

■

There will be no ordering of poppers,
jalapeno or otherwise.

■

There's no need to ask for her number—unless you are romantic
and misguided. (One exception: You both currently live in the same city.) Like
airport seafood, airport romance is better left to people who don't know better.

■

Never ask a stranger to watch your bag.
It's not that you don't trust him. He just has better things to do, like being free to
leave whenever the spirit—or boarding announcement—moves him.

■

Always pay cash.
You may not have time to wait for that credit-card slip.

TAXIS

'ROUND THE WORLD

LONDON

Tip: Round up to the whole pound, or 10 percent.

Exit cab and pay outside. For an unmetered minicab, ask for fare beforehand.

MILAN

Tip: Round up to the nearest euro.

Usually found at a taxi stand, rarely hailed on the streets, but they might stop if empty.

OSLO

Tip: No tipping required.

But taxi drivers expect a small tip if they handle heavy luggage. Everything costs a lot because the service is built in.

NEW YORK

Tip: 10 to 15 percent.

For unmetered livery cabs, ask for fare beforehand. For yellow cabs, the center light on means available; the center light off means taken; and if the two lights flanking the center light are illuminated, it's off duty.

PARIS

Tip: Not usually given.

But for outstanding service, a euro or two is fine. Cars occasionally stop when hailed, but mostly you have to queue at a stand.

CAIRO

Tip: 5 to 10 percent.

Solo men sit in front with the drivers, solo women in back. Black-and-white cabs are unmetered hoopties. Yellow cabs are metered—and air-conditioned—but hard to track down on the street. Try to book by phone.

MOSCOW

Tip: 10 percent.

Price negotiated with driver or set beforehand; no meters. It's highly recommended that you not take a gypsy cab, and either find a taxi in front of a hotel or phone one up.

JETIQUETTE

···

THE RULES OF CIVIL BEHAVIOR AND DISCOURSE AT 35,000 FEET

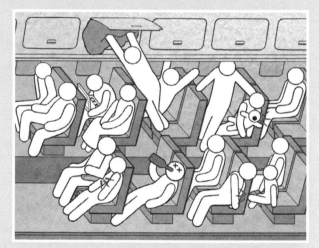

1. You're sitting near a screaming baby: Not much you can do. Try earplugs or headphones to drown out the noise.

2. You're sitting near a screaming/kicking child: If he's ruining your flight, ask the parents if they can tell their child to stop whatever it is he's doing. Say please and thank you when asking, and if that doesn't work, inform the flight attendants. They will take it from there.

3. You want to spread your legs: draw an imaginary line from your armrests to the armrests of the seats in front of you. Don't let your knees cross those lines, and don't let anyone else's, either.

4. Your neighbor wants to spread his legs: If he looks like a leg spreader, mark your territory by positioning your knees just inside the imaginary lines you've drawn. If your neighbor's knees knock against your knees, do not cede an inch. It should take only a few moments of touching knees to sufficiently shame him back into his own space.

5. You're having a cocktail: Drink enough to relax, and keep your voice low.

6. You're watching a movie on your computer. If it involves "adult situations," position your player's screen at an angle so that you alone can see it.

7. You've got a carry-on: Don't wheel your bag behind you down the aisle—instead, carry it in front of you until you get to your seat. Try to stow it in an overhead bin in the general vicinity of your seat. (One row forward and one row back is fair game.) Wheels in first, handle out.

8. You've got a window seat and you need to use the bathroom: Exit facing the front, with your back to your neighbors.

9. You want the armrest: If you're sitting in a window or aisle seat, you already have one armrest all to yourself. When it comes to the middle armrest, the elderly, women, and children get first dibs.

If, however, none of those apply or you're sitting in the middle seat, it's first come, first served. If one or both armrests are already taken, try reclining your seat all the way back and positioning your elbow behind your neighbor's.

TRAVELING MISTAKES
A MAN SHOULD NEVER MAKE

- **WEARING** a neck pillow at any moment you are not attempting to sleep.

- **TRAIPSING** to the plane's bathroom in your socks. You've seen those floors.

- **SITTING** in the aisle seat of a train to deter someone from sitting next to you.

- **RECLINING** your seat farther than you truly need to be comfortable.

- **ATTEMPTING** to prevent the person in front of you from fully reclining his seat. Yes, you're tall. Not his problem.

- **CONCERNING** yourself with whether or not liquids are out of your carry-on and in a separate plastic bag for security. No one does this anymore.

THE NE'ER-DO-WELL'S GUIDE TO TRAVEL

YOU'VE BEEN HURT

YOU'VE BEEN ARRESTED

YOU'VE LOST YOUR PASSPORT

DON'T PANIC: Assuming you have any control over your situation—i.e. you haven't been hit by a bus or need immediate attention—do not head to the nearest hospital. (They may not provide adequate care.)

DO YOUR RESEARCH: Return to your hotel and ask the concierge for a good, reputable hospital in the area. If you don't trust your concierge, call your embassy.

RECONSIDER YOUR PLANS: If your injury requires a second opinion or follow-up, think about cutting your vacation short.

SIGN NOTHING: even if it's in English, you might not be fully aware of the paperwork's implications.

SAY AS LITTLE AS POSSIBLE: Especially if there's a language barrier. Whatever you say probably won't help your cause, because, well, you've already been arrested.

GET HELP: Ask politely but firmly to speak to a representative from the nearest U.S. embassy or consulate, who can get you a lawyer and explain exactly what's going on. And until that person arrives, again, say nothing.

GET ORGANIZED: Assemble any alternate evidence of your identity: driver's license, credit cards with your name, photocopies of your passport.

HEAD TO THE EMBASSY: And if you've got a friend who can vouch for you (and who still has a passport), bring him along. He may be able to expedite the process.

DRESS UP: Embassies are constantly suspicious of U.S. citizens selling their passports for quick cash, so you might have an easier time if you don't look like a bum.

JUST SAY **NO**

WHERE YOU'LL FIND THE HARSHEST DRUG LAWS,
FROM EXTENSIVE JAIL TIME TO DEATH SENTENCES

	DEATH PENALTY	JAIL TIME
CHINA	☠	
INDONESIA	☠	
IRAN	☠	
LAOS	☠	
MALAYSIA		🔗
MOROCCO		🔗
OMAN	☠	
PHILIPPINES		🔗
SINGAPORE	☠	
SAUDI ARABIA	☠	
SRI LANKA	☠	
THAILAND	☠	
TUNISIA		🔗
UNITED ARAB EMIRATES	☠	
VIETNAM	☠	

THE GRATEFUL MAN

How to say "please" and "thank you" in five different languages

	PLEASE	THANK YOU
ARABIC	Min fadlak (*meen fad-lak*)	Shukran (*shook-ran*)
GERMAN	Bitte (*bit-eh*)	Danke (*dahnk-eh*)
PORTUGUESE	Por favor (*poor fuh-vor*)	Obrigado (*oh-bree-gah-doh*)
JAPANESE	Kudasai (*koo-dah-sah-ee*)	Domo arigato (*doh-moh are-ee-gaht-oh*)
SWEDISH	Tack	Tack

-TIPPING-

PEOPLE YOU **SHOULD** TIP	PEOPLE YOU SHOULD **NEVER** TIP
Valet: $5	**Cops.**
Car-wash guy: $3.	**Doctors.**
Coat check: $2 an item.	**Teachers.**
Hotel porter: $3 a bag.	**Wives.**
Barista: $1 or $2, if she smiles.	**Mall Santas.**
Housekeeping staff: $5 a day.	
Skycaps: $5. (Note: if you tip them $20, they might upgrade your luggage to first-class status to ensure your bag comes out of the belt first.)	

A GESTURE'S WORTH AT LEAST TWO WORDS

Simple ways to express your displeasure, no matter your location.

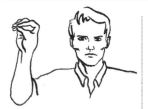

WHEN IN FRANCE:
Raise your hand in front of you as you bring your thumb and fingers together.

WHEN IN PORTUGAL:
With your palm facing outward, extend your index and pinkie fingers while holding down the others with your thumb.

WHEN IN PAKISTAN OR GREECE:
Hold an open palm with fingers splayed toward your victim, as if you were a mime.

WHEN IN THE MIDDLE EAST OR WEST AFRICA:
Thumbs-up. Not as encouraging over there.

WHEN IN INDIA OR KOREA:
Point your index finger and straddle it with the index and middle fingers of your other hand.

ANYWHERE ELSE:
Draw your finger across your throat. Shake your head slowly if you are feeling particularly nefarious.

HOW TO CARE FOR

YOUR VACATION BEARD

(NO MATTER HOW LONG YOUR VACATION)

2-3 DAYS
Wash and moisturize normally.

1-2 WEEKS
Apply baby oil to ease itching.

3-4 WEEKS
Tidy up by shaving a sharp neck line.

8-12 WEEKS
Shampoo and condition often.

12-18 WEEKS
Feel free to get creative with styles.

24-48 WEEKS
Brush regularly to remove tangles.

1 YEAR
Check beard after eating and remove crumbs.

A LIFETIME
Learn to play guitar, start ZZ Top cover band.

CHAPTER SEVEN

AT THE OFFICE

WHAT I'VE LEARNED

Ambition is exhausting.
It makes you friends with people for
the wrong reasons, just like drugs.
—CARRIE FISHER

If they think we got an edge,
we got an edge.
—RED AUERBACH

THE RULES

RULE NO. 619:
No one finds out you're a tea drinker
until after you've got the job.

RULE NO. 633:
At the office holiday party, consume
one drink fewer than your boss.

RULE NO. 699:
Say hi to the interns.

HOW TO **INTERVIEW FOR A JOB**

➤ A suit, and a tie, and shoes that were shined that day.

➤ Don't be late. But don't be too early, either. Six minutes, max. Any more and you become an interrupting weenie.

➤ What to carry: a notebook and a pen in your breast pocket; your resume (even if they already have it); mints; a little confidence.

➤ Don't bring a briefcase. No reason you'd need one, except to try to look important. Also, if possible, avoid wearing an overcoat. One less thing to worry about.

➤ Stand, don't sit, in the waiting area. Less fussing with yourself when they come to retrieve you.

➤ If it's not obvious where you should sit for the interview, just ask. Try something like, "Where's a good place for me to sit?"

➤ When you speak, tread in the waters that lie between the shores of braggadocio and self-deprecation.

➤ Which means that you can toot your own horn a little. Never assume someone has memorized your resume. Or looked at it.

➤ The same day: Mail a thank-you note. In the mail. **The actual mail**.

- YOUR FIRST DAY -

Don't bring doughnuts.

Say very little.

Smile a lot.

Don't call any meetings.

If no one invites you to lunch, don't take it personally.

Remember for them it's just another day at the office.

Ask where you can find a decent sandwich,
and wash it down with your tears.

THE WAY OF

THE HANDSHAKE

THE HANDSHAKE SHALL BE FIRM, FAST,
AND FREE OF EXCESS PERSPIRATION.

TRANSLATION: **Firm** meant a squeeze, but not a hard squeeze.

Fast means that this squeeze happens in an instant and is not sustained.

As for **perspiration**, that was discreetly wiped off on your trousers
a few seconds ago.

HOW TO **DATE AT WORK**

(ABRIDGED)

The chances of it all working out are slim.

✿

That said, it happens.

✿

Your relationship will remain secret for no more than three weeks,
no matter how hard you try—and you must try.

✿

The good news: no one will really care.
At least not after the first day or two.

✿

The only real problem is when one of you is the other's boss.
You could maybe get fired.

✿

Don't bring your work home with you.

✿

Conversely, no canoodling, bickering, or lovemaking at the office.

✿

Exit strategies are limited to a job change and marriage.

✿

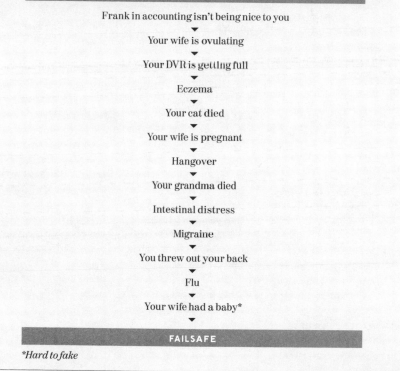

CALLING OFF WORK
A CONTINUUM OF POSSIBLE EXCUSES

RISKY

Frank in accounting isn't being nice to you
▼
Your wife is ovulating
▼
Your DVR is getting full
▼
Eczema
▼
Your cat died
▼
Your wife is pregnant
▼
Hangover
▼
Your grandma died
▼
Intestinal distress
▼
Migraine
▼
You threw out your back
▼
Flu
▼
Your wife had a baby*
▼

FAILSAFE

*Hard to fake

THREE O'CLOCK

IN THE CONFERENCE ROOM

BASIC RULES FOR NAVIGATING AN OFFICE MEETING

- **Be the second or third** person to a meeting. Never first and never last.

- And then, **choose your seat** as if you were choosing a urinal, being aware of proximity to others.

- **Every once in a while**, be the guy who sits next to the boss.

- **What you need** for every meeting: something to write on, something to write with.

- **What you do not need**: a drink, your cell phone, your assistant.

- **ALWAYS:** Take notes on paper.

- **SOMETIMES:** Take notes on an iPad.

- **NEVER:** Take notes on an envelope, index card, or other strange object you're convinced makes you look creative.

- **Can you see** what your colleague has written on his notepad? Good for you. Stop reading it.

- **Only the boss** gets to put his phone on the table.

- **Which is to say,** only the boss can check e-mail and texts.

- **No one can check** his Twitter feed.

- **No raising your hand.**

- **Always stick up** for yourself, but remember, you rarely benefit from blaming others.

- **On a conference call,** you can push the mute button only once to make fun of another participant on the call. After that, it's just annoying.

- **Everybody knows** you tried to deflect

that question by asking another. Still, sometimes it's all you've got.

- **The lowest-ranking** person in the room always takes the most notes.

- That said, **interact with your coworkers** as if you all have the same title.

- **If you're making a presentation,** you are more than welcome

to simply read the text from the slides. Especially if you don't expect people to pay attention.

YOU'VE BEEN FIRED

- **ASK IF THE DECISION IS FINAL.** Do not plead. If the decision is final, it is final. Respect it.

- **ASK IF YOU CAN RESIGN INSTEAD OF BEING TERMINATED.** In searching for a new job, it is better to have left voluntarily that to have been fired. If the firer agrees, ask: "If I were to resign, would you agree not to contest my unemployment claim?" (Employees who are fired or laid off can collect unemployment benefits, but those who resign usually have to petition for it.) If they agree, be grateful; if they do not, accept the firing for the sake of securing unemployment.

- **DO NOT BAD-MOUTH ANYBODY.**

- **THEY MAY OFFER TO MAIL YOU YOUR STUFF** so you can leave quickly and quietly, or they might give you the rest of the day to say goodbye and clean out your desk. Go with the latter. A man does not sneak away.

- **NO MATTER WHAT YOU DO, BE CONCISE AND GRACIOUS WITH EVERYONE.** "Great working with you, good luck, keep in touch."

- **DO TRY TO KEEP IN TOUCH.** The best way to find a new job is through the recommendations of former coworkers.

CHAPTER EIGHT

MAINTENANCE
(HEALTH & GROOMING)

WHAT I'VE LEARNED

Smoke like a chimney, work like a horse, eat without thinking, go for a walk only in really pleasant company.
— ALBERT EINSTEIN

Three meals a day. Work hard. Keep yourself clean. Get enough sleep. What else is there?
—ANTONIO PIERRO

THE RULES

RULE NO. 707:
If you are uncertain how much cologne is enough, you are not allowed to use cologne.

RULE NO. 727:
You should never be subjected to looking at a man's toes.

RULE NO. 734:
There is so much a mustache says about a man. And none of it is good.

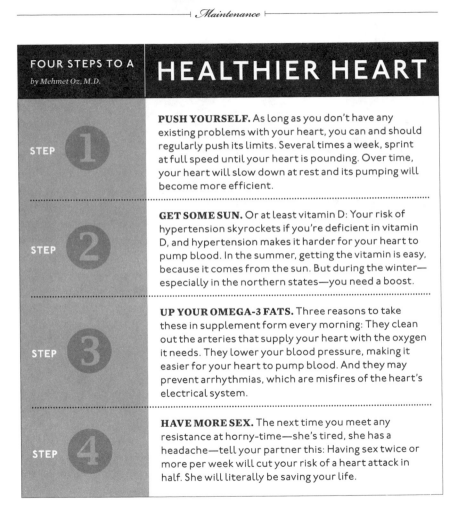

FOUR STEPS TO A
by Mehmet Oz, M.D.

HEALTHIER HEART

STEP 1

PUSH YOURSELF. As long as you don't have any existing problems with your heart, you can and should regularly push its limits. Several times a week, sprint at full speed until your heart is pounding. Over time, your heart will slow down at rest and its pumping will become more efficient.

STEP 2

GET SOME SUN. Or at least vitamin D: Your risk of hypertension skyrockets if you're deficient in vitamin D, and hypertension makes it harder for your heart to pump blood. In the summer, getting the vitamin is easy, because it comes from the sun. But during the winter—especially in the northern states—you need a boost.

STEP 3

UP YOUR OMEGA-3 FATS. Three reasons to take these in supplement form every morning: They clean out the arteries that supply your heart with the oxygen it needs. They lower your blood pressure, making it easier for your heart to pump blood. And they may prevent arrhythmias, which are misfires of the heart's electrical system.

STEP 4

HAVE MORE SEX. The next time you meet any resistance at horny-time—she's tired, she has a headache—tell your partner this: Having sex twice or more per week will cut your risk of a heart attack in half. She will literally be saving your life.

THE MAINTENANCE CHECKLIST

☐ **ONCE A MONTH:**
RESTING PULSE

Take your heart rate when you first wake up or after five minutes of lying down. If it's over 75 beats per minute, you can cut your risk of having a fatal heart attack in half by slowing it down to fewer than 60 beats per minute. To do that, aim to regularly speed it up with exercise.

☐ **ALSO ONCE A MONTH:**
PULSE RECOVERY

Measure your pulse while doing any exercise that gets your heart thumping at its maximum rate. Then rest for one minute and measure again. If the difference isn't 12 beats per minute or greater, your risk of death—death!—in the next six years is twice as high as it should be.

☐ **ONCE A YEAR:**
BLOOD PRESSURE

This is easy to check at either your regular doctor's appointment or using the little machine in the local pharmacy. If the top number is 120 or less, you're in good shape. If it's over 140, you have hypertension and probably won't make it to the end of this article. If it's between 120 and 140, you have pre-hypertension—doesn't sound horrible, but in fact it means your risk of a heart attack is still three and a half times higher than it should be. Get that number down by exercising, cutting your salt intake, and taking vitamin D and omega-3 pills.

☐ **ONCE EVERY FIVE YEARS:**
CHOLESTEROL

Cholesterol isn't a problem for only old men who eat a lot of eggs. High levels in your twenties or thirties double your risk of a fatal heart attack later.

☐ **ONCE:**
GET AN EKG

Most doctors don't routinely perform EKGs on healthy men, but once you hit middle age—forty, say—it's worth asking for one. Minor abnormalities in your heart's electrical circuits may not cause any symptoms, but they can signal an increased risk of heart disease.

FOUR STEPS TO A
by David Perlmutter, M.D.

HEALTHIER BRAIN

STEP 1

EAT MORE FISH. Or increase your intake of DHA, a type of omega-3 fatty acid that's found in fish and is also available in capsule form as a vegetarian supplement. Studies show that 900 to 1,200 mg of DHA a day could lead to improved memory and a better ability to multitask.

STEP 2

CHECK YOUR FOOD LABELS. When you eat bad fats (i.e., trans and saturated fats), you're building brain cells from the lowest bidder, and it'll slow down the brain's ability to process information quickly. Conversely, mono-unsaturated fats (from olive oil, canola oil, and nuts) and polyunsaturated fats (from cold-water fish and deep-green vegetables) help improve brain function.

STEP 3

LEARN A NEW LANGUAGE. Or memorize a poem, or do crossword puzzles. Challenging yourself through mental exercise builds a better brain by reinforcing brain-cell connections.

STEP 4

MEDITATE. In a book called *How God Changes Your Brain*, Andrew Newberg, M.D., shows how twenty minutes of daily meditation can alter the brain structurally and therefore functionally. Changes in key areas allow us to be more compassionate and empathetic, and they allow us to handle stress a little better.

THE MAINTENANCE CHECKLIST

THE NEXT TIME YOUR DOCTOR TAKES BLOOD, ASK HIM TO TEST
FOR THE FOLLOWING INDICATORS OF BRAIN HEALTH:

☐ **ONCE A YEAR:**
BLOOD PRESSURE

Homocysteine is to the brain what cholesterol is to the heart, and an elevated level compromises brain function and dramatically increases a person's risk for Alzheimer's.

☐ **ONCE A YEAR:**
C-REACTIVE PROTEIN,
which is a marker for inflammation in the body. Its presence in your blood shows you're at risk for brain degeneration.

☐ **ONCE A YEAR:**
SLP, OR SERUM LIPID PEROXIDE,
which is a measurement of how well your antioxidants are working. Antioxidants protect the brain, and the less functional they are, the more at risk you are for brain degeneration.

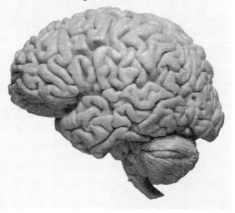

FOUR STEPS TO
by Harry Fisch, M.D.

HEALTHIER BALLS

STEP 1

LOSE THE BELLY. If you decrease the size of the pubic fat pad—that's the fat that sits right above the penis—it will make your penis look longer (which you probably don't care about) and will boost your sex drive (which you probably do). Testosterone is normally broken down in the body's fat cells, and abdominal fat breaks down testosterone extra quickly and leads to testosterone deficiency. By losing the belly fat, you'll increase the amount of testosterone in your system and feel the difference in the bedroom.

STEP 2

DO MORE SQUATS. By doing exercises concentrated below the waist, you can increase the blood flow in your pelvic region, and that, in turn, can increase the width of the penis. Not a lot, but still.

STEP 3

EAT MORE WALNUTS. Or almonds. Or anything that contains an amino acid called arginine, which is also found in beans, cold-water fish (tuna, salmon), soy products, and oats. Arginine promotes a process called nitric-oxide release, which relaxes blood vessels and increases the blood flow to the penis. You can also find arginine in dietary supplements like L-arginine—though don't exceed more than 2,800 mg in a day.

STEP 4

GET SERIOUS ABOUT LOWERING YOUR CHOLESTEROL. Among the myriad other reasons for doing this: It will facilitate blood flow to your penis and impact your sex drive, the girth of your penis, and the firmness of your erection.

THE MAINTENANCE CHECKLIST

☐ **EVERY DAY:**
PAY ATTENTION

Does it burn when you pee? Are you seeing blood? Is there any discomfort when you adjust yourself? If the answer is yes and the problem lasts for more than a few days, see a doctor.

☐ **EVERY SIX MONTHS:**
CHECK YOUR BALLS

Feel around your testicles for hardness and discomfort, and If you sense anything that feels like a knuckle, see your doctor. There's a chance it could be testicular cancer.

☐ **ONCE A YEAR:**
GET A PHYSICAL

And ask your doctor about your blood pressure, cholesterol, and testosterone levels. If you're having problems with any of those things, it'll eventually influence your sex life. Good heart, good penis.Good penis, good heart.

THE *HURRIED MAN'S GUIDE TO*

ANGER

THE UPSIDE

If you're feeling challenged or threatened, signals in your brain tell the adrenal glands on top of your kidneys to start pumping cortisol, adrenaline, and other catecholamines into your bloodstream. When the adrenaline reaches your heart, it beats faster and gives you the rush you need to conquer fears and take action.

. . . AND THE DOWNSIDE

When these biological events are triggered by irrational thoughts instead of actual threats, anger can morph into rage. Or what technically is known as IED, Intermittent Explosive Disorder. When a guy's IED goes off, he loses control, something gets smashed or broken, or someone gets hurt or threatened. It wreaks havoc on your home and work life and may up your risk for heart disease and high blood pressure.

THE *HURRIED MAN'S GUIDE TO*

ANXIETY

THE UPSIDE

Say you're putting final touches on a presentation. You're tensing up, and your stomach's a little upset, but you still feel you've got things under control. This is a normal reaction to stress, and it's exactly what's needed to motivate you to do your best.

. . . AND THE DOWNSIDE

Say you're giving the same presentation, but you don't feel in control—you're panicking, you can't focus, and you even consider avoiding the meeting altogether. That is anxiety gone haywire, and it's painful and unproductive.

So what causes it? Anxiety is always related to the brain or, more specifically, the amygdala, which is responsible for processing and storing memories associated with emotional events—including anxiety and the "fight or flight" response. People with an overactive amygdala may have a heightened response to fear, which can cause increased anxiety, dramatic spikes in blood pressure, and damage to you heart and kidneys.

THE *HURRIED MAN'S GUIDE TO*
DEPRESSION

THE UPSIDE

In the same way physical symptoms are your body's way of letting you know that something's wrong, depression can be your mind's way of telling you that you need to deal with a psychological problem. Plus, many people who change their habits to relieve their symptoms of depression end up feeling better than they did before they became depressed.

. . . AND THE DOWNSIDE

There's the guy who experiences depression as it's commonly known—feels hopelessness, worthlessness, and yes, very, very tired—and then there's the guy who's working sixty-hours a week, being short-tempered with his coworkers, and drinking too many martinis at lunch. Good chance he's experiencing depression, too.

The exact causes are unknown—low levels of serotonin in the brain are commonly cited, as are unresolved traumas from your past—but depression has been proven to have a direct link to heart disease—the leading killer of men.

TOOLS FOR GOOD HEALTH

PREVENTION

....

HOW TO KEEP ANGER, ANXIETY, AND DEPRESSION AT BAY THROUGH EVERYDAY HABITS

■ **GOOD SLEEP:**
Research shows that people who go without enough good sleep (generally considered at least six hours a night) are up to six times as likely to become depressed as those who get good sleep.

■ **GOOD SEX:**
Levels of the "Happy neurochemicals" serotonin and endorphin have been found to rise in post-orgasmic rats. At the same time, there's a surge in oxytocin—which is believed to reduce stress levels—as well as an uptick in prolactin, thought to be associated with the sleepy feeling after sex. These findings suggest that having sex (or taking matters into your own hands) brings some temporary relief for stress or anxiety.

■ **GOOD EXERCISE:**
Particularly aerobic exercise. The best evidence to date—based on the analysis of fourteen random controlled trials—indicates that to prevent, and even effectively treat, depression with exercise requires three thirty-minute sessions per week of aerobic exercise at 60 to 80 percent of maximum heart rate (i.e., typically between 110 and 160 beats per minute) for at least eight weeks.

■ **GOOD FOOD:**
Up your intake of omega-3 fatty acids and vitamin B12, both of which show promise in contributing to mental well-being. Tuna, mackerel, and salmon are good sources for omega-3 fatty acids, as are dark green vegetables, flaxseed, nuts, and soybeans. For sources of B12, look to seafood and low-fat dairy products. Carbs have also been found to raise the level of serotonin in your brain, but it's best to stick with low-fat, whole-grain sources.

■ **ALCOHOL:**
Take it easy and limit it to the standard two drinks a day.

YOU GONNA EAT **THAT?**

WHETHER YOU'RE TRYING to put on muscle or just live to see your 60s, one of the most important things you can do for yourself is eat right. (And change the batteries in your smoke detector, but now we're just nagging.) Here, a brief guide to acceptable foods.

THINGS YOU SHOULD EAT [1]
Fish, eggs (with the yolk), vegetables, milk-based proteins, oatmeal, brown rice, sweet potatoes.

THINGS YOU CAN EAT [2]
Beef, chicken, pork, fruits (they're high in sugar and carbs), breads (whole wheat), cereals, white rice, potatoes.

THINGS YOU SHOULDN'T EAT [3]
Bagels, doughnuts, beer, liquor, and everything else that tastes good.

[1] You can never go wrong with plants. Or (lean) protein.

[2] Even natural sugars and whole-wheat carbs present some dangers. Enjoy in moderation.

[3] The fewer ingredients you recognize in something, the less likely you should eat it.

A (*Healthier*) DAY AT THE BEACH

*WHAT WERE ONCE RELAXING ACTIVITIES
CAN NOW BECOME PARTS OF A RIGOROUS FULL-BODY WORKOUT.*

  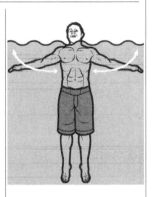

❶ **WHEN YOU TOSS** a football, do it in shallow water. The resistance works your legs harder.

❷ **PLAY SPORTS LIKE** Kadima or volleyball on the dry sand for a better calf-and-foot work-out. Use your non-dominant hand. This will challenge your brain (and your ability to throw like a man).

❸ **GO OUT IN** the water where you can't touch. Tread water using only your arms.

THE VAGUELY INTERESTED

MAN'S GUIDE TO THE GYM

1. Check in. Be sure to grab a towel. Smile!

2. Start with at least five minutes of cardio to warm up.

3. A treadmill at incline 12.0 and speed 3.5 burns as many calories as running.

4. Weight machines operate on fixed planes, so they're less likely to cause an injury. If you don't really know what you're doing, start here.

5. Never block a weight rack or a person's view of the mirror (often used to monitor form). It's just rude.

6. It's perfectly acceptable to ask the nearest person for a spot.

7. It should be common sense, but still: If you're filling a water bottle, let the guy behind you grab a drink first.

8. Stationary bikes can be great for cardio, but only if you really push yourself. Which is to say, you shouldn't be able to read a magazine.

9. In the locker room: Keep eye contact, banter, and requests for mole checks to a minimum. And don't forget flip flops.

THE
WORKOUT RULES

~ RULE NO. 321 ~
The length of your running shorts should be directly proportional
to the average time it takes you to run a mile.

~ RULE NO. 403 ~
There is no comfortable way to spot someone doing squats.

~ RULE NO. 471 ~
No flexing.

~ RULE NO. 488 ~
Before you offer someone weight-training advice,
walk the other way and keep it to yourself.

~ RULE NO. 510 ~
The arm bike is for rehab only.

~ RULE NO. 511 ~
The leg-abductor machine is for women only.

~ RULE NO. 539 ~
No matter how long the run you just finished on the treadmill,
you should never point your fingers to the sky
in thanks or celebration.

IF YOU CAN SPARE ONLY 20 MINUTES A DAY...

Do the following circuit 3 times, resting 1 minute between rounds,
and watch the pounds come off.

....

• AIR SQUATS, 1 min

....

• PUSH-UPS, 1 min

....

• BENT-OVER DUMBBELL ROWS, 1 min

....

• BURPEES, 1 min

....

• DUMBBELL SHOULDER PRESS, 1 min

....

HOW TO BE OUTSIDE

SOLUTIONS TO OUTDOOR SITUATIONS A MAN MAY FACE IN THE SUMMER.

THE SUN IS OUT: Unless you had horrible parents, we're not the first to tell you: Put on sunscreen. You want one that protects you from UVA rays, which age your skin, and UVB, which cook it. The American Academy of Dermatology recommends an SPF of at least 30, applied 15 minutes before going outside and every two hours after that. And don't forget your scalp. A few hair products even have SPF built in.

THE SUN IS NOT OUT: Clouds block as little as 20 percent of UV rays. See above.

A MAN HAS ASKED YOU TO "GET HIS BACK": If the man is a stranger, it's best to move on. If not—and if there's no one around with whom he might have a closer relationship—oblige him. You may need the favor repaid at some point.

YOUR DEODORANT DOESN'T SEEM TO BE WORKING: As discreetly as you can, dry your armpits with something you won't need again: A paper towel or someone else's T-shirt. Removing the sweat reduces smelly bacteria.

YOU HAVE A HAIRY BACK: If it's a special occasion (honeymoon, work picnic, reality-TV audition), four weeks before any expected disrobing, visit a spa for a wax. A few days after, scrub your back with a washcloth to limit clogged pores and breakouts, which look a lot worse than a back full of hair.

YOU PLAN ON GOING BAREFOOT: You need only two things—a pumice stone and some moisturizer—and two minutes of effort. Use the pumice stone to rub the dead skin from your heels, then apply moisturizer. And trim your nails. If you see any signs of fungus, do the right thing: Wear shoes.

SOMEONE MENTIONS YOUR CALF IMPLANTS: Soak up the attention.

SUNSCREEN

WILL SUNSCREEN STAIN MY CLOTHES?
Dermatologists recommend avoiding anything with avobenzone, which, when mixed with certain minerals in water, can leave rust-brown stains on clothes.

ARE SPRAYS AS EFFECTIVE AS CREAMS?
Yes, if you're especially thorough. A spray is easier, but it delivers less sunscreen than a cream. If you consider yourself sun sensitive, you should probably stick with the creams.

TRUE OR FALSE: THE THICKER THE CREAM, THE BETTER THE SUNSCREEN.
True, in general. But only because thicker creams are harder to spread, which ends up making you apply more.

WHY ARE SUNSCREENS ALWAYS WHITE?
According to the Skin Cancer Foundation, it's the ingredients. Compounds like titanium dioxide and zinc oxide are white in nature. For a long time, they were opaque and paste-like and wouldn't absorb into the skin. Most sunscreens now use cosmetically refined particles that absorb straight into your skin with little residue.

IS IT OKAY FOR A MAN TO SMELL LIKE COCONUT?
If someone has spilled a pina colada on him, yes. Then and only then.

A BRIEF GUIDE TO

RESPONSIBLE TANNING

First, think twice about it. Even responsible tanning can be dangerous, and you've got other options. Look into sunless tanning solutions like lotions, creams, and sprays. It's the only safe way to get a tan, and you have to reapply only every couple weeks.

If you really have to be in the sun, though, use an SPF 30 with broad-spectrum UVA and UVB protection and reapply every two hours. Spend no more than 20 or 30 minutes in direct sunlight at any given time, and avoid spending too much time in the sun between noon and four. (The midday sun is the worst for you.)

Build a tan over a period of weeks, not days, and apply moisturizer daily to avoid the dry, scale-like skin that often follows a tan.

SO YOU'RE **SUNBURNED**

START BY TAKING A COOL BATH.

This will reduce the temperature of your skin and provide some temporary relief—and take two pain relievers (aspirin is best) every six hours. If you have blisters, clean them with hydrogen peroxide, then apply an over-the-counter antibiotic ointment like Bacitracin two or three times a day until the blisters dry out. Do not puncture or otherwise attempt to open the blisters if they're not ready.

YOU CAN ALSO TRY THE FOLLOWING HOME REMEDIES:

COLD MILK:

Pour cold milk into a bowl and soak a few paper towels in it. Place them on the affected areas; the milk will soothe the skin and function as an anti-inflammatory agent, its coolness will lower the skin's temperature.

WETTED AND CHILLED TEA BAGS:

Apply directly to the burned or blistered area. The coolness will lower the skin's temperature, while the tea bags' tannic acid will help to dry out the blisters and reduce swelling.

VINEGAR AND WATER:

Take a capful of vinegar and mix it in a small bowl of cold water. Soak paper towels in the mixture and lay the sheets over areas with blisters that you're afraid may become infected. Like tea bags, the vinegar has a drying effect.

AN ILLUSTRATED GUIDE TO

TAN LINES

AND WHAT THEY SAY ABOUT YOU

You are a farmer.

You drive with your windows down. And you probably have a huge carbon footprint.

You're unfaithful to your wife. Or you're at least trying to be.

Your Cartier Ballon Bleu is in the shop. (Even if you really just wear a Casio G-Shock.)

LIGHTNING ROUND: **SUMMER FEET**

When it's time for beaches, flip-flops, and finally caring for those things
you usually hide in shoes, we don't begrudge you a few questions.

I don't want pretty feet, just unembarrassing feet. What should I be doing?

You probably already know to cut your toenails straight, leaving just a sliver of white at the top. Rounding them like you would your fingernails leads to ingrown toenails, then pain. Maybe pus. Once a week, remove any calluses or dry, dead skin with a pumice stone or foot file. It'll take a minute. Two, tops. (If you have diabetes, podiatrist Dr. Jeffrey DeSantis suggests leaving the exfoliation to your doctor, since poor circulation can dull sensation and prevent you from noticing when you've scraped too far.) And try a little lotion when you get out of the shower. You'll keep your heels from looking cracked—and maybe stop snagging your sheets.

Lotion?

Yes, lotion. Get something with peppermint. It smells nice.

What about me? I want pretty feet.

Consider the professional pedicure: calluses scraped down, ingrown toenails removed, skin softened through various soaks and ointments. Plus, you get a foot rub. Just ask them not to buff your nails, which tends to look like you got a coat of clear polish. One warning: some salons don't properly disinfect between customers, which can lead to fungal infections. If you're particularly worried about this, DeSantis recommends investing in and bringing your own tools.

Is there anything I can do about my sweaty feet?

Like two to three percent of Americans, you could be suffering from hyperhidrosis. It's not a big deal. DeSantis recommends washing your feet thoroughly with antibacterial soap and dusting them with Gold Bond to remove excess moisture. You can also switch from cotton to synthetic socks, which wick sweat away instead of absorbing it. If that doesn't work, try antiperspirant. It blocks sweat glands on your feet just as it does under your arms. Or there are always Botox injections, which last several months and can cost upwards of $1,500.

Why are toenail clippers so much bigger than fingernail clippers?

Because your toenails are bigger. And thicker. Also, the flatter arc of toenail clippers allows for a straighter, easier cut.

Why don't I get little white dots on my toenails like I do on my fingernails?

You do. They're just less common and harder to see.

Do I really need flip-flops to take a shower at the gym?

Yes. Unless you like athlete's foot.

Why do fingernails grow so much faster than toenails?

Nobody knows, but scientists speculate fingernails receive greater blood flow, since they are closer to your heart.

Warts are contagious?

Sure are. Warts, which you are likelier to contract if you already suffer from germ-festering conditions like athlete's foot or hyperhidrosis, can be passed on through direct or indirect contact (like that gym shower you were so blasé about). DeSantis says the warts on your feet are caused by a strain of the human papilloma virus—the same virus that causes genital warts.

How do I get rid of this hard little knot of skin on the bottom of my foot? It doesn't usually hurt.

It's probably just a callus, which can form due to excessive pressure. If it doesn't bother you, leave it alone. If you decide you don't like it, you can scrape it down with a pumice stone, but if it's deep, see a professional.

My girlfriend left her nail brush in the shower. Is there any real benefit to this thing?

Nope. DeSantis says nail brushes do nothing for you, and using someone else's puts you at risk of catching a fungus.

Anything else I should be aware of?

Don't forget sunscreen. Every year DeSantis notices an increase in melanoma on feet as more people wear flip-flops. Nothing ruins beach time faster than skin cancer.

HOW TO GO BAREFOOT WITHOUT SHAME

CORNS AND OTHER UNSIGHTLY MARKS:	DISCOLORED NAILS:	CALLUSES AND DRY PATCHES:
INVEST in over-the-counter foot-care remedies—Dr. Scholl's products remain the gold standard—and if, after following the directions on the packaging, you don't see any improvements, get thee to a podiatrist. Do not, under any circumstances, attempt to remove corns on your own.	USE small scissors to trim the corners of your toenails so that the surrounding skin can breathe. Then, three to four times a week, apply tea-tree-oil drops to those same corners to keep the area clean and free of fungus.	PURCHASE a pumice stone from a pharmacy and, before showering, scrub around the side of your foot where skin is flaky or cracked. After showering, spread Vaseline on your heels. For optimal moisture, once a week before bed, cover your feet in Vaseline, put on athletic socks, and remove when you wake up.

A FEW WORDS ON HAIR TOES

Don't panic. You're a man, after all. Your feet will have **hair** on them, and the few times a year you break them out in **public**, those who can't look up should look away. If it **really bothers you**, you can have your feet **waxed**, or even get **electrolysis**, which'll run you a couple hundred dollars and hurt like hell. The easier choice is to grab a set of **beard trimmers** or **snub-nosed scissors.** Every **couple of weeks** or the day you're planning on going to the pool, **trim a bit.** Not too short. **Think rough**, not putting green.

HOW TO **GET THE STANK OUT**

SHOE TREES

Cedar shoe trees help shoes retain their shape, but they also give them a chance to dry out by absorbing any accumulated sweat into the wood. (For this reason, always choose a porous wood, never varnished.) Germs thrive in moisture, so when you reduce moisture, you reduce germs. And when you reduce germs, you reduce odor. Which lets you take your shoes off without apologizing.

DEODORIZERS

They're not a permanent solution, as they don't actually do anything to reduce all that festering, but deodorizers do cover smells with a pleasant alternative. Twist one open and put it in your shoes or a gym bag—or anywhere else in need of an olfactory boost. Maybe in the kitchen after your next batch of signature pork and sauerkraut.

DEODORANT

It works on your feet just like it does under your arms. Roll on a deodorant to add a better scent, or an antiperspirant to block the sweat glands entirely.

TEA

That's right, tea. The tannins kill bacteria. Just remember to let it cool first.

THE *BEGINNER'S GUIDE TO*

NOSE MAINTENANCE

TO REMOVE EXCESS NOSE HAIR:

Take a warm shower to moisten up the hairs, and then position yourself in front of a well-lit mirror. Holding a small pair of eyelash scissors at a 45-degree angle to your septum and with your head tilted slightly back, begin snipping away at only those hairs you can see in the mirror. *Don't insert the scissors into your nose any more than absolutely necessary* and don't turn up your nose to get hard-to-reach hairs. If you can't see it poking out of your nose, leave it be.

Or invest in an electronic trimer and save yourself the anxiety.

TO CLEAR UP LARGE PORES AND BLACKHEADS:

Open up your pores by applying a warm towel to your nose for about ten minutes. Then apply an exfoliant with buffing grains and massage gently for two minutes before washing clean. Moisturize.

HAIRCUTS

FOR THE AGING MAN

THE PROBLEM	THE SOLUTION
RECEDING TEMPLES	**A finger-length cut** roughly an inch all over your head. At that length, the recession at your temples won't be quite so noticeable. *See also:* Justin Theroux
THINNING CROWN	**Grow everything out** about an inch, keeping the hair around your balding spot slightly longer than that on the rest of your head. That little bit of extra hair will go a long way to compensate for the emptiness up top. *See also:* Hugh Laurie.
OVERALL THINNING	**This here's the purgatory** of hair loss—you still have a full head of hair, but it's so thin that your scalp is clearly visible from certain angles. You can buzz it all off, as many do, or you ask to have it layered and cut forward, without a part. *See also:* Michael Bolton
SEVERELY RECEDING HAIRLINE AND/OR THINNING CROWN	**You don't have** a ton of good options. Your best bet: Ask your barber to blend from the thin spots to the corners, making sure there's a smooth transition from scalp to hair. *See also:* Kelsey Grammer
TOTALLY BALD UP TOP, A LITTLE BIT OF HAIR ON THE SIDES.	**Two options here.** You can either pull out the razor and shave the whole head down to the skin (which may, if you do it right, convey to others that you're buzzing your head by choice, not out of necessity), or you can own your baldness by keeping the hair on the sides and making sure it's tidy. *See also:* Jim Cramer

THE POWER OF **SIDEBURNS**

YOUR FACE IS PERFECT. REALLY. BUT IN CASE YOU STILL HAVE CONCERNS, A FEW EASY FACIAL-HAIR FIXES FOR COMMON ISSUES.

1. ROUND FACE.
Grow your sideburns about three-quarters of the way down your ear to give your face the illusion of length. Thin them out near the ends instead of having a sharp line.

2. NARROW FACE.
You want sideburns that end somewhere between the top and middle of your ear. Too long and you risk looking like a harnessed horse.

3. BOXY FACE.
Don't square the bottom, which just reinforces your face's geometry. Let them grown down and taper off naturally. An extension of your hair—as opposed to your beard.

4. ANY KIND OF FACE PAIRED WITH LONG HAIR.
If your hair is longer than five inches, you don't want sideburns at all. Unless you enjoy looking like a ramblin' man.

THE UPKEEP OF SIDEBURNS

Comb or push them toward your nose. Anything outside the sideburns' normal outline should be trimmed. Use beard clippers. Or those little scissors your wife always has in the medicine cabinet.

HOW TO MAINTAIN

A MAGNIFICENT BEARD

If you're man enough to grow a beard, you sure as hell better be man enough to maintain it. And you can't whine about the work: Two wet shaves and a clipper trim each week are all it takes to keep things from going the way of Grizzly Adams.

TWICE A WEEK: Hop into the shower to soften up the scruff. Then apply shaving cream to your cheekbones just over the sides of your beard, along your neck from the collarbone up to below the jaw, and in the space between your nose and the top of your 'stache. Wet-shaving these areas will define the lines of your beard.

ONCE A WEEK: Following a wet shave, rinse and dry your face, and pull out your clippers. Be sure to get a set that's adjustable and has guards so that you have flexibility in terms of beard length. Because you've already cleaned the lines of your beard, you're just making sure your beard is consistent in length and thickness.

AFTER WET SHAVE OR CLIPPER TRIM : Thoroughly rinse your beard and work with your fingertips to get cleansers and moisturizers into the skin beneath it. Be lazy about it and a world of skin problems await come spring when you opt for a clean shave.

HOW TO **TREAT YOUR FACE**

THE ATTENTION YOU GIVE YOUR FACE doesn't depend on how often you're in the sun or the kind of free radicals you're exposed to. Well, it should, but it doesn't. Your grooming regimen depends on one thing: you. Whatever your level of grooming interest—high, moderate, or Vince Vaughn—at some point in your life you'll need to find a balance between what your face needs and what your personality can tolerate. Take a look at the three basic categories below. Find the one that best describes you, and with it you'll find a suitable combination of creams, cleansers, and maybe even a serum. Adapt at will. Follow. Repeat.

THE DANDY	Follows a strict routine. Never forgets to floss. Has skin that's been referred to as "supple." Unintimidated by places most men fear (spas, bed-and-breakfasts, Jamba Juice). Familiar with the word *unguent*. Likes brunch. *SUGGESTED REGIMEN:* 1,2,3,4,5,6,7,8,9,11
THE DABBLER	Has tried toner but still doesn't know what it does. On occasion applies cologne directly from a magazine. Willing to use a pumice stone, but only if his girlfriend buys it for him. Defines ironing as hanging a shirt near the shower. Owns tweezers. Hides them. *SUGGESTED REGIMEN:* 2,3,4,5,9
THE SKEPTIC	Sees aging as a way to improve his looks. Doesn't understand why people wash jeans. Surprised by women who don't find calluses appealing. Unfamiliar with fabric softener. Has referred to the application of deodorant as "showering." Occasionally carries an ax. *SUGGESTED REGIMEN:* 2,4

THE REGIMENS

1. Facials.
Life—especially smoking, drinking, and being stressed—shows up in your skin. Monthly facials not only clean and rehydrate, they clear your pores, allowing them to release perspiration and toxins.

2. Moisturizer (morning).
Find something with a strong, penetrating element like glycerin.

3. Moisturizer (evening).
Applying again at night helps make the next morning's shave less irritating.

4. Face wash (morning). Use something with a cooling agent, like aloe, mint, or tea-tree oil, to calm any irritation.

5. Face wash (evening).
Women do it to remove makeup. You should do it to remove a day's worth of dirt.

6. Serum.
Applied before your moisturizer, serum can increase collagen production and minimize wrinkles—and discretionary income.

7. Toner.
A complement to face wash. Provides a deeper clean. Applied by cotton ball or, even more embarrassingly, mist.

8. Eye cream.
The skin around your eyes is the thinnest on your face, and thus the first to dry out. Eye cream can prevent dark circles and can help reduce the bags that show up when you're not sleeping enough.

9. Exfoliating scrub. The slight abrasiveness removes dead skin cells, letting your moisturizer penetrate. Or just shave. It's a similar exfoliating process.

10. Enzyme peel.
Enzymes are just exfoliating agents, giving you a deeper cleanse than a scrub by digesting the dead skin on your face. NO thanks.

11. Mask.
A minifacial, only cheaper and around fewer women.

12. Placental face cream.
Apparently has great proteins and antioxidants. You first.

THE (*Precisely*) SCENTED MAN

FOR CLOTHING, IT'S RELATIVELY SIMPLE:

You wear what the situation dictates. Which means no tuxes at the beach, no collarless shirts at the golf club, and—unless you happen to drive a UPS truck—no shorts at the office.

EVEN SIMPLER IS THE RULE FOR COLOGNE:

Buy one and wear it when you want to smell good. At least that's how it used to be. Now there are so many, with such subtle nuances, you could have a specific cologne for every situation you'll ever face. In case you're into such things, or if you just want to be adequately informed before making your next purchase, we prepared this handy guide (opposite).

SITUATION	CALLS FOR
THE JOB INTERVIEW	**A CITRUS-BASED FRAGRANCE.** Citrus molecules are so light that they can be used only as top notes—the first thing you smell when you smell cologne. Within 60 minutes of application, they'll have dissipated completely, leaving only a subtle, musky undertone.
THE BIG PRESENTATION	**A CHYPRE.** It's a combination of the fragrance families— woody, citrus, and oriental—which means it's a big, powerful, impression-leaving scent. Which also means you should be even more careful than usual not to over apply.
THE BRUNCH WITH MOM	**A FOUGERE.** It often contains lavender and oak moss, giving it a fresh, classic smell, kind of like your dad's aftershave (so long as he was using good aftershave). A fougere will make her subconsciously proud of the man you've become.
THE ANNIVERSARY DINNER	**A WOODY FRAGRANCE.** This type of cologne is heavier, so it lasts longer and hangs closer to the body, requiring intimacy to be noticed. She won't smell it unless she leans in.
THE HOTEL BAR	**AN ORIENTAL FRAGRANCE.** Like woody scents, orientals hang around all day. But they're a little more potent and hard to ignore. You'll catch occasional whiffs of yourself. Others will, too.
THE WEEKEND AWAY	**NOTHING.** Subconscious feelings of attraction are triggered when the right mate smells your natural scent. Still, take a shower.

WORDS AND PHRASES A MAN CAN USE
TO DESCRIBE HIS COLOGNE

WOODY, WOODSY,

SPICY, PEPPERY,

WARM, FRUITY,

JUST LIKE GRANDPA'S,

LIGHT, BOLD, NUTTY,

GREEN, CLASSIC,

SUBTLE, EVOCATIVE,

FRESH, MOSSY,

PUNGENT, MUSKY,

SHARP, GOOD.

AND A FEW HE CANNOT

AN EXPERIENCE,

JUST LIKE GRANDMA'S,

THE AURA OF AGARWOOD SPIKED BY TONKA BEAN,

DESIGNER IMPOSTER,

ME.

CHAPTER NINE

COMPETENCE
(HOW TO GET THROUGH LIFE)

WHAT I'VE LEARNED

Being a Baptist won't keep you from
sinning, but it'll sure as hell
keep you from enjoying it.
—JIMMY DEAN

I don't know what it is about the
shower that generates creative
thoughts. Maybe it's the hot water.
Maybe it's being unencumbered even
by the restriction of clothing.
—LYLE LOVETT

THE RULES

RULE NO. 818:
Never play cards with a man
who wears a visor.

RULE NO. 864:
You might have tweeted your
condolences, but you still
have to send flowers.

RULE NO. 871:
Before you make fun of the
crest on a man's jacket,
make sure it's not for his dojo.

HOW TO

CHEAT AT POOL

WHEN YOU'RE RACKING, **nudge the head ball**

to create space between it and the rest of the rack while the

opponent isn't watching. He'll get a horrible break. **Also:** When

he's not looking, **wet the tip** of your opponent's cue.

The tip won't hold chalk until it dries out, and his next shots will

miscue—his **shots won't go anywhere**.

HOW TO WIN THE GAME

WITHOUT COMING OFF LIKE AN ASSHOLE

GOLF	TENNIS

GOLF

➤ A little light gambling is devoutly to be desired. Gets everyone focused.

➤ Early in the round, give your opponents a few three-footers. Makes you seem like a nice guy but doesn't let them get comfortable with the short putts. The four-footer on 17 with $50 on the line will look a whole lot longer.

➤ Praise but don't go overboard. "Golf shot" is plenty.

➤ Every time your opponent tees off on a par-3 shout, "I've never seen one! Oh, my God, I've never seen one!" It's either really funny or it will drive him to distraction.

➤ During the round, there's never a bad time to buy everyone a drink. If there's money on the line, you don't have to actually, you know, drink.

➤ Act like you don't want their money when they're settling up.

➤ Enjoy your drink. Talk about how well everyone played. Commiserate over that putt on 17.

TENNIS

➤ Two cans of balls. Don't be the dick who shows up empty-handed.

➤ Ignore your friend's foot-faulting. Ninety-four percent of recreational players foot-fault. It's just part of the game.

➤ Line calls you make: If it's close, it's in.

➤ Line calls he makes: Third bad call, walk halfway to the net, peer toward the spot the ball landed, then walk back to the baseline and resume play.

➤ A little light cursing is fine, shows you care, suggests that you are trying. Unless there are children on the next court.

➤ No throwing the racket. If you must, a racket dropped with just the right measure of disgust is every bit as effective.

➤ As Red Auerbach once said to Charlie Pierce, "If you're keeping score, win."

➤ And then buy the beer.

HOW TO **FELL A TREE**

TOOLS: *CHAIN SAW, PROTECTIVE EYEWEAR, COMFORTABLE SHOES*

❶ DETERMINE THE DIRECTION OF FALL, remembering that a leaning tree gives you no choice in the matter. Plan a path of retreat for when the tree begins to come down and clear any obstacles in that path. Make your first cut parallel to the ground, a third of the way into the tree on the side facing the direction of fall.

❷ MAKE A SECOND CUT downward from above at a 60-degree angle, stopping when you meet the first cut. Remove the wedge of wood thus formed. This is the face cut, and it will guide the tree as it topples.

❸ MOVE TO THE OPPOSITE SIDE OF THE TRUNK. With your blade parallel to the ground and positioned one to two inches above the bottom of the face cut, saw horizontally into the trunk but not all the way. Your aim is to leave a "hinge"—a strip of uncut trunk about an inch thick and parallel to the back of the face cut. The hinge keeps the tree from twisting and kicking back as it falls.

❹ AS YOU COMPLETE THE HINGE, the tree will likely begin to topple. Switch off the saw and make your retreat. Don't run and don't turn around to watch. Once you hear the thud, it's safe to stop and look.

HOW TO

JUMP START A CAR

....

TOOLS: *JUMPER CABLE, GOOD SAMARITAN*

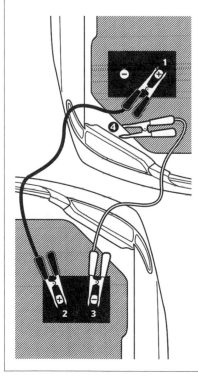

❶ Shut off the running car's engine and pop both cars' hoods.

❷ Remove the rubber caps protecting the terminals atop each battery. Identify the positive and negative terminals. (If the + and – symbols have been obscured somehow, note that the negative terminal is almost always connected directly to the car's frame by a short, black cable. The positive terminal is usually connected by several colored cables to various parts of the engine.)

❸ Connect the jumper cables in this order: dead-battery positive to good-battery positive; good-battery negative to the engine block or frame of the dead-battery car. (Connect to raw metal only, not painted or otherwise coated.)

❹ Start the good car and let it run for about five minutes, then try to start the dead car. If this fails, try again in another five minutes. If it still doesn't work, the battery is beyond help. Call a tow truck.

❺ Disconnect the cables in the reverse order that you connected them.

– 137 –

YOU'RE ON A BOAT!

What you should say, wear, and expect to see swinging across the deck the next time you're invited for a day of yachting.

- Listen to the captain. **Always.** Treat the boat like it's someone's home (it probably cost as much) and realize things can be dangerous if you're not paying attention.

- If you can't make it, let the captain know as soon as possible. Especially if you're expected to help crew the ship.

- If you're staying overnight, pack light and bring soft luggage. (It compresses easier.) There's not a lot of space on a boat, and you don't want to take up any more than you have to.

- Don't forget your sunglasses.

- Wear white-soled, nonmarking, nonskid shoes. You know, boat shoes.

- To avoid staining your host's deck, bring white wine, not red.

THE UNIFORM

- When the ship turns or tacks in the wind, be ready for the mainsail to swing across the deck.

- Learn how to tie a cleat. (See page 141.) You might be asked to help secure the boat upon docking.

- While under way, the rule is simple: one hand for you, one for hand for the boat.

- Ask before smoking. And make sure no one's downwind.

- Sound carries more easily over water, so watch what you say about the nearby boaters.

- Ship toilets can be confusing. And easy to break. Ask for directions before using one.

- Oh, and call the ship toilet the "head." It only feels funny the first time.

- Say thank you.

HOW TO

DOCK A BOAT

➤ Before you do anything, you need to understand how a boat moves. (It's best to practice in open water, where no one can see you — and where you're less likely to hit something.)

➤ You can make the boat turn in two different ways. In forward gear, turn the wheel the direction you want the bow (front) to go. In reverse, turn the wheel the direction you want the stern (rear) to go.

➤ Now that you're confident, approach the dock at a 15 degree angle (wider if the wind or current is moving away from the dock, depending on how strong it is).

➤ As the bow is about to touch the dock, turn the wheel hard toward the dock and put the engine in reverse. This will pull the bow out—keeping it from hitting—and suck the stern into the dock.

➤ Tie up the stern, short and tight, then shift into neutral. Straighten the wheel and shift into forward very briefly. This will bring the bow closer to the dock.

➤ Tie off the bow and shift into neutral.

➤ Get out of your boat.

HOW TO
TIE A CLEAT

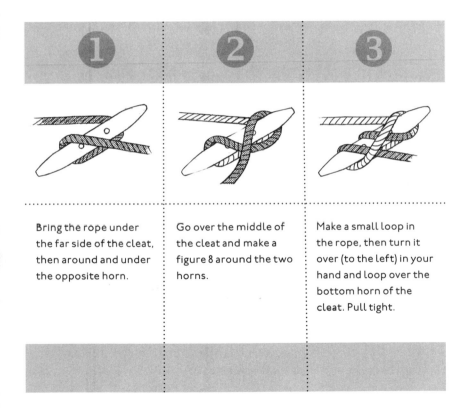

①	②	③
Bring the rope under the far side of the cleat, then around and under the opposite horn.	Go over the middle of the cleat and make a figure 8 around the two horns.	Make a small loop in the rope, then turn it over (to the left) in your hand and loop over the bottom horn of the cleat. Pull tight.

HOW TO **REMOVE A STRIPPED SCREW**

Rubber band

First, try a wide rubber band.

———

Lay one side of it flat on the damaged screw head,
then press against it with your screwdriver.
Often that will get you enough purchase to remove the screw.

———

If that doesn't work and you can't get hold of the screw head
with pliers, find a small torx screwdriver.
(It's the one that look like a star and comes with most screwdriver sets.)

With a drill bit slightly smaller than the torx,
drill about ½ inch into the screw.

———

Pound the torx in with a hammer.

———

Unscrew.

———

Celebrate.

HOW TO **TUNE A BIKE**

What to do before your first ride of the season

A CHECKLIST

☐ **Check for dry, cracked patches** on the tires and brake pads. Replace if found.

☐ **Fill your tires.** The recommended pressure is usually inscribed on the side of the tire.

☐ **Lube the chain.** Flip your bike upside down and, as you pedal backward with your hand, drip a chain lube like Tri-Flow on the inside of every link. Shift through all gears, then remove excess lube by holding a rag lightly around the chain as you pedal. Repeat.

☐ **Check your brakes.** Pull on the brake levers. Hard. They should stop halfway to the grip, and then you should be able to squeeze them just a little bit more. If they go all the way to the grip, turn the barrel adjuster (it looks like a nut at the start of the brake cable) counterclockwise. Move the smaller locking nut tight against the brake lever.

☐ **True the wheels.** Spin each wheel, looking to see if there are any slight bends. When you find a bend, tighten or loosen the spokes near it: If the rim bends left, tighten the spoke that goes into the right side and loosen the one that goes into the left. Squeeze both spokes to even out the tension.

HOW TO

FIX A LEAKY FAUCET

1. Under the sink, you should see two metal knobs on the wall. They control the water line. Turn them off.

2. Back above the sink, look for a cap on the hot- and cold-water handles. Pop it off with a utility knife or screwdriver to expose a screw.

3. Remove that screw to remove the handle.

Packing nut

Seat washer *O-ring*

4. If you're lucky, all you'll need to do is tighten the packing nut — the hexagonal nut beneath the handle.

5. If that doesn't work, remove the packing nut. In a newer sink, you'll find a one-piece cartridge. Take it to the hardware store, get a replacement, and install it. You're done. In an older sink, under the nut is a stem with an O-ring and a seat washer, held in place by a screw. Changing the O-ring will usually stop a leak in the handle. (Make sure you get the right size.) Drips from the faucet, however, are often caused by corroded seat washers. Whichever you need, coat the replacement in plumber's grease before you install it. If you don't have a new washer handy and the unused side of the old washer is smooth, sometimes you can just flip it over.

6. If the dripping continues, run your finger inside where the stem rests in the base of the handle. If you feel rough patches, you can try using an abrasive pad to smooth them down. Or just replace the part. Tell the guy at the hardware store you need a new valve seat. He'll know.

7. Reassemble everything and enjoy your sink.

HOW TO
SEW A BUTTON

TOOLS: *NEEDLE, THREAD*

❶ TAKE TWELVE INCHES OF THREAD, knotted securely at one end, and thread your needle. Make a single stitch in the shirt in line with the row of buttons, about ⅛ inch long, and then make another stitch perpendicular to the first.

❷ HOLD THE BUTTON about ⅛ inch away from the shirt and thread the needle up through one hole in the button and down the diagonally opposite hole. Do the same with the other holes and then repeat four times.

❸ WRAP THE THREAD TIGHTLY around the ⅛-inch shank that has been created between the button and the cloth to create a tight pillar.

❹ PUSH THE NEEDLE THROUGH this pillar a few times and cut the thread close to it.

❺ BUTTON UP.

HOW TO

SHINE A SHOE

....

TOOLS:

TIN OF WAX-BASED POLISH,
WELT BRUSH, POLISHING CLOTH,
HORSEHAIR BUFFING BRUSH, OLD TOOTHBRUSH

❶

Wipe down your shoe with a damp cloth and scrub out
the welt strip with a damp welt brush.

❷

Apply polish sparingly with the polishing cloth (an old sock
wrapped around two fingers works perfectly) using a circular
rubbing motion. For the "spit-shined" look, you can dip the
cloth in water, which helps the polish stuff the leather. The
more you rub, the better, until it develops a waxy, matte
finish. Let the polish dry for about five minutes.

❸

Buff the entire shoe with a buffing brush for about
five minutes longer than you think sensible.
For extra gleam, hold the shoe between your knees
and buff the toe with a clean cloth.

❹

Use a toothbrush to apply polish to the welt and edge of the
heel. Dust off any excess polish with the buffing brush.

HOW TO **LOOK GOOD IN A PICTURE**

Find a picture of yourself **that you like** (or that your wife likes) and study it.

Notice the way you're holding your head, the way your body is positioned. Those are the **angles that work** for you.

Nobody looks their best looking straight into the camera, so **drop your chin** a bit and/or rotate your face a few degrees to either the left or right. This will add definition to your jawline.

Try putting your feet together, with your **left leg forward** and bent a little at the knee and your right leg slightly back with the knee locked. Then rotate your hips (but not your feet) slightly to your right or left— 15 degrees is plenty. This should make you look taller, thinner, and stronger.

Don't forget to **smile**.

HOW TO BE BETTER LOOKING

STYLE

- Buy clothes that fit. (For non fitted shirts you already own, tuck them like hospital corners: Pinch the seams on the side and pull them back while tucking the excess underneath for a tapered look.)

- Wash it. Press it. Tuck it in. Then forget about it. Never enter a party thinking, How do I look? Enter thinking, Here I am.

- Pay attention to dress codes. One man's free spirit is another man's self-centered git.

- Get a tan. Always look as if you just got back from somewhere interesting and expensive. It worked for Onassis.

—ESQUIRE *FASHION DIRECTOR*
NICK SULLIVAN

PICTURES

- Put one foot slightly behind the other, centered with your spine. It forces you to stand up straight.

- Lower your chin and rotate your face slightly. It'll give you a strong jawline. Or the appearance of one, at least.

- Opt for soft lighting.

- Position the camera (or camera-person) so it's shooting at a slightly downward angle.

- Use a telephoto lens; it flattens faces (and noses) and generally makes everything look more beautiful.

CONFIDENCE

- Look people in the eye. According to Gordon Patzer, attraction expert and author of *Looks: Why They Matter More Than You Ever Imagined*, people are most attractive to others when they're looking directly at them.

- Pay attention to body language. Patzer says that crossing your arms—or any sort of closed-off body language—makes you look less attractive.

- And stand up straight. It'll do wonders.

HOW TO **BE MORE INTERESTING**

IT'S ALL IN YOUR CONVERSATION

SOME RULES

➤ Listen more than you talk.

➤ If you notice yourself getting bored with what you're saying, stop talking. Acknowledge the situation. Smile. Move on.

➤ Know a few historical anecdotes. Like this one: To enhance creativity, surrealist painter Salvador Dali recommended afternoon naps lasting less than a second. He would lie in his chair, arms outstretched, holding a metal key in his left hand. As he drifted off to sleep, his grip would relax and the key would fall, clanging onto a plate he'd set beneath it and waking him up.

➤ But realize that no one likes the guy who knows something about everything.

➤ Let people talk over you. Don't think of it as being rude; think of it as an assist.

➤ If someone does interrupt you, wait to be prompted before continuing your story. It's a good sign that someone cared in the first place.

➤ Drawn-out pauses are the best time for personal non sequiturs. People would rather listen to you talk about yourself than nothing.

➤ With people you don't know, limit stories to the last five minutes of your life—the turnout, the Scotch selection, the homeless man you mistakenly took for a valet.

➤ Never mention your blog.

HOW TO NEVER GET ANGRY

According to heart surgeon and author Dr. Mehmet Oz, empathy can be an effective palliative. Understanding why someone screwed you, even if you have to make it up, makes it harder to be offended. Just keep embellishing until you feel better.

AN EXAMPLE:

Someone cuts you off in traffic.

POSSIBLE EXCUSE:

He's late for a flight.

⬇

That'll take him to a funeral.

⬇

For his only daughter.

⬇

Who died trying to rescue his wife.

⬇

From a fire that burned down the cabin
he built with his father.

⬇

Where she was staying with her new lover.

⬇

Who turned out to be his best friend.

HOW TO **SHARPEN YOUR OWN KNIVES**

*NB: If the knife you want to sharpen has a serrated blade,
stop reading this and take it to a professional. Otherwise:*

❶ **Go to the hardware store** and buy a two-sided sharpening stone. It'll run you ten to twenty bucks.

❷ **Mark the edge** of the dull blade with a felt-tip marker. That way, if the line isn't disappearing, you'll know you're not holding the knife at a consistent angle — or making any real progress. Wet the coarser side of the stone with water or oil.

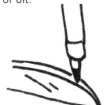

❸ **With one hand** on the knife handle and two or three fingers of the other hand resting on the blade for support, hold the blade 20 degrees off the

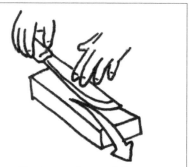

stone (flat is zero degrees). Starting with the tip, slowly push the knife across the stone.

❹ **Repeat** until the marker line is gone and you see a burr — a slight overhang extending from the sharpened side. Switch sides and repeat. After a new burr is formed, flip the stone to the finer side and make a few additional strokes at a slightly higher angle to hone it away.

HOW TO **BE YOUR BEST** ON COMMAND

SKIP

BEFORE A BIG MEETING, a stressful situation, the chance to beat your mom at Yahtzee—anytime you need to come through in the clutch, find a way to skip. Jim Fannin, a performance coach who's worked with guys like Alex Rodriguez and Carlos Delgado, says that it's hard to skip without laughing, even if it's at yourself. Laughing adds endorphins to your bloodstream. Endorphins calm you down. Being calm reduces your stress. Reduced stress allows you to regain focus.

HOW TO **BOUNCE BACK** ON COMMAND

CLOSE YOUR EYES.

....

LOWER YOUR CHIN

and think about whatever's making you upset.

....

RAISE YOUR CHIN

to the sky, and open your eyes.

....

BY DOING THAT, Fannin says,

75 percent of people forget about whatever was bothering them,

whether it's a strikeout or someone seeing them skip.

HOW TO

BE TALLER

HANG FROM DOORFRAMES all you want. Once you're done growing—typically in your late teens—there's really only one way to make yourself taller: yoga.

According to Alex von Bidder, a New York City yoga instructor, one to two years of basic yoga can get you up to an inch in height— simply by making you stand straighter. He recommends the following poses, two to three times a week. We recommend not turning into one of those guys who carries around his own yoga mat.

MOUNTAIN POSE

(Separates vertebrae, aligns spine.)

Feet just inside shoulder width, tailbone tucked toward your heels, belly button sucked in. Move your shoulder blades back and down. Stretch your head up toward the ceiling. Hold for one minute.

DOWNWARD-FACING DOG

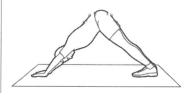

(Strengthens, draws back shoulders.)

Begin on all fours with your hands just in front of your shoulders. Lift your knees off the floor, straighten your legs, and push your heels toward the floor. Breathe deeply for one minute.

SIMPLE SUPPORTED BACKBEND

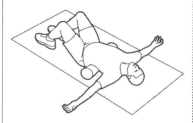

(Provides a deep, supported stretch.)

Lie back with a cylindrical pillow just below your shoulder blades and a rolled-up blanket beneath your neck. Open your arms, palms facing up. Breathe deeply.

SIMPLE RECLINING TWIST

(Tones torso, balances spine.)

Tuck your chin slightly. Arms open, palms up. Breathe in and bring your knees to your chest, then, as you exhale, lower your legs to the right side. Breathe deeply for one minute. Repeat on the left side.

HOW TO **TELL THE DIFFERENCE**

Between a RED-TAILED HAWK
and a TURKEY VULTURE

*Because mistaking a scavenger for a graceful hunter
just makes you look silly. To some people.*

RED-TAILED HAWK | TURKEY VULTURE

PROFILE: Both have broad wings and a rounded tail, but the vulture's wings will appear more boxy and rectangular. Also, when seen head-on, a hawk's wings will make a straight line; a vulture's wings will be tilted up in a distinctive shallow V shape.

FLIGHT PATTERN: Both birds rarely flap their wings, preferring to soar in wide circles. A vulture, however, will appear to wobble back and forth in flight.

THE BASICS OF GAMBLING

Know the vocabulary.

SPREAD: The number of points a team is favored or not favored by, indicated by a minus sign (next to the favored team) or a plus sign (by the underdog).

COVER: To win by more than the spread.

TAKE THE POINTS: To bet that the underdog will lose by less than the spread.

CHALK: The favorite. (To "go chalk" is to bet the favorite.)

OVER/UNDER: Predicted total number of points in a game. "Over" means you think the teams will score more than predicted. "Under" means less.

Always take the under in championship games. Most people take the over, betting more on what they

want to see than on what they think will happen. Sports books know that and raise the totals a little higher than they should be.

It's never a bad idea to take the ugly underdog. Betting on a team no one likes means you're essentially playing with the sports book—especially in marquee games with a lot of bettors. Sports books make money for a reason.

HOW TO

CALM A CRYING BABY

First of all, don't get all bent out of shape.

◆

Accept that they baby's feelings are legitimate.

◆

The infant must perceive your empathy and calm
and feel absolutely confident in it.

◆

Hold the baby close and walk around.
Use the body heat from your torso and a lilting motion,
moving at about the speed of a heartbeat.

◆

Speak in a low bass voice with a measured cadence
close to the baby's face.

◆

Recite something. Like W.B. Yeats's poem "The Stolen Child."
Or the lyrics to Bob Dylan's "Just like Tom Thumb's Blues."

◆

If a few minutes of this treatment doesn't calm the baby,
the only thing that will is breasts.

◆

Which you don't have.

A GUIDE TO USING

IMPORTANT PEOPLE

	Virtue	Expectation (Reasonable or not)	Tip?
TAILOR	A good eye	Compensating for your body's natural shortcomings. Performing miracles.	Nope. It's part of the fees.
BARBER	Reliability	Quietly adjusting your regular cut to fit your receding hairline. Making that receding hairline go away.	Fifteen to 20 percent of the bill, or three to five bucks if it's just a trim.
CADDIE	Prescience	Knowing which club you need at the exact moment you need it without your having to ask for it. Grabbing you a beer from the snack shack.	Twenty bucks for 18 holes with a young caddie, $50 to $100 with an experienced one.
SHOE SHINER	Affability	A good shine, a sunny disposition, rapid brush skills. Making cheap shoes look like anything more than cheap shoes.	Two dollars on a five-dollar shine.
BARTENDER	Wisdom	The occasional buyback. Listening to your drunk rambling all night long.	If you're running up a tab, 15 to 20 percent of the bill. If you're paying by the drink, one or two bucks per drink.
PERSONAL ASSISTANT	Discretion	Lying to your boss or wife about your availability. Lying to a grand jury.	Cash at the end of the year.

THE CULTURALLY RESISTANT MAN

HOW TO PREPARE FOR, AND BEHAVE IN, HIGH SOCIETY

AT THE GALLERY

How to Prepare:
It's important to understand the artist's context. Many museums offer lectures on their artists, which you could attend. At the very least, read the brochure.

How to Enjoy:
Focus on a couple of rooms. The longer you study a painting, the more details you'll notice. Look for those details that trigger a response. If you aren't sure what's good about a piece, ask the staff. It's why they're there.

How to Discuss:
Talk about whatever moved you, either emotionally or intellectually. If you don't like something, don't be scared to say so. Just be sure to explain your logic (too garish, simplistic, etc.).

How to Dress:
Comfortably. People should be looking at the paintings, not at you.

AT THE BALLET

How to Prepare:
You can read up on the story to get a little background if you want, but it's not necessary.

How to Enjoy:
Look for energy from the performers. When in doubt, watch their feet. And if someone happens to fall, it's customary (if counterintuitive) to clap a little longer for them after the performance.

How to Discuss:
Talk about how the dancer drew you into her world, how precise the movements were, and whether it looked like she was living out the music or dancing separately from it.

How to Dress:
Khakis and a nice shirt. If you're feeling fancy, throw on a blazer.

AT THE SYMPHONY

How to Prepare:
Orchestras often provide program notes or podcasts on their Web sites ahead of time. Read and listen to them.

How to Enjoy:
It's perfectly acceptable to close your eyes. Or track the melody by watching whom the conductor points to. *One warning:* Orchestras pause at the end of every movement. Clap only at the end of each piece (when the conductor turns around).

How to Discuss:
Talk about how it made you feel—happy, sad, worked up. Music should be about emotional response. Share yours.

How to Dress:
No need for black tie, but you want to look nice. Dress as if you were meeting your in-laws at a nice restaurant.

AT THE OPERA

How to Prepare:
If you learn the story in advance, you'll spend less time reading the subtitles and more watching the singers. And don't make your first opera Wagner. Starting opera with Wagner is like learning to read with *War and Peace*.

How to Enjoy:
Try to physically feel the voice of the singer filling the concert hall. She's not miked. Really fast or heavily dramatic passages are the most impressive. If you fall asleep and miss the end, assume that the main characters died. They usually do.

How to Discuss:
Some vocabulary: An aria is usually sung by one person. More than one person, it's an ensemble. Diva (divo for men) is a perfectly normal way to refer to a singer. As is prima donna (the lead).

How to Dress:
Cocktail attire. No cape.

THE CONSIDERATE MAN

IN THE BEDROOM

♦ No clothes on the floor. Dirty stuff in the hamper, put the rest away.

♦ Hahaha. But seriously: Go ahead and throw your clothes on the floor, but only in the area immediately surrounding your side of the bed. Nobody will trip on them but you.

♦ Acceptable things to do in bed: Sleeping, reading, watching TV, having sex, and, if necessary, the discreet breaking of wind.

♦ Unacceptable things to do in bed: eating, smoking, clipping nails, engineering a Dutch oven for her presumed enjoyment.

♦ One hit of the snooze button: fine. Two hits: really?
Three or more: dick.

IN THE KITCHEN

♦ The scratching of one's ass is a pleasure best enjoyed outside the kitchen.

♦ It is better to finish something off completey than to leave one sip of milk or the butt of the bread loaf.

♦ Shirt when cooking? Recommended. Pants.? Required.

♦ You: Take out the garbage. Fix appliances when broken. Clear table. Her: Wipe down counters. Sweep floor. Clean out fridge. Everyone: Buy groceries. Do dishes. Cook.

♦ Sit down to eat. Barring that, over the counter or sink. Pick up crumbs any larger than a grain of rice. Forget about the rest.

IN THE BATHROOM

◆ No. I: Toilet seat up. Barring that, don't piss on the seat. Barring that, wipe it up.

◆ No. 2: Flush and, when in doubt, flush again. Light a match or, if it's there, a candle.

◆ Should your wife or partner befoul the bathroom: polite silence, or possibly an innocent joke.
Note: "Damn, woman, what'd you eat?" is not an innocent joke.

◆ Brushing teeth, shaving, possibly even showering if it's just you and the missus: Door can remain ajar. Anything else: Shut it firmly.

◆ Showers: under ten minutes, fifteen tops.

◆ Beard whiskers in the sink, patches of toothpaste here and there: totally fine.

◆ Nobody, save said missus, needs to see you naked.

IN THE WORK RESTROOM

◆ Always: Flush.

◆ Sometimes: Use the middle urinal.

◆ Never: Pee in the stall. That's the equivalent of showering in a bathing suit.

◆ And for chrissakes, don't throw paper towels on the floor simply because you'd rather not touch the door handle.

THE RULES OF OVERNIGHT GUESTS

YOU'RE THE HOST	YOU'RE THE GUEST
• Fresh sheets. Clean towels on the edge of the bed.	• Arrive on time. If you'll be more than 15 minutes late, call to let them know.
• Unless they were involved in your birth or that of your wife, let them find their own way from the airport.	• Don't show up empty-handed. Try Sequoia Grove Napa Valley cabernet sauvignon (safe) or Vieux Pontarlier absinthe (adventurous).
• Stock the fridge. Beer, milk, eggs, maybe a few cheeses. Humboldt Fog and aged Gouda are nice.	• Unless you are out with your hosts, you should be home by 11. Not everyone's on vacation.
• You're not a tour guide, but you do know the lay of the land. Share it. But only if they ask.	• Things you should always offer to do: wash the dishes, strip the sheets.
• Have a spare set of keys handy. It'll help your guests feel less like they're inconveniencing you.	• If you wanted to sleep late, you should have splurged on a hotel. Get up when you hear others are awake.
• Always be the first one up.	• Send a thank-you note.
• No sex.	• No sex.

APPROPRIATE WAYS OF SAYING

THANK YOU

*You've stayed the weekend,
and now you're wondering how to show your gratitude.
That all depends on who your hosts are and
whether you want to be invited back.*

	FRIENDS	PARENTS	HOTEL
TEXT	passable	unadvised	unadvised
CALL	passable	ideal	unadvised
NOTE	ideal	passable	unadvised
TIP / PAYMENT	unadvised	unadvised	ideal
GIFT	ideal	passable	unadvised
NAME OF FIRSTBORN	unadvised	passable	unadvised

HOW TO

FEIGN ENTHUSIASM FOR A GIFT

Look for one thing that you like about the gift.
The color, maybe, or how soft it is, or how useful
the person who bought it thinks you'll find it.

✳

Say thank you, then mention the aspect you like.

✳

If the gift giving continues to another person,
examine your gift until the next gift is being opened or
until 30 seconds have passed. Whichever comes first.

✳

Set it carefully beside you.

✳

Maybe get caught looking at it one more time.

HOW TO

TELL SOMEONE IS FEIGNING ENTHUSIASM FOR A GIFT

Watch the corners of their lips, their cheeks, and their eyes.
All three should rise at the same moment.

✳

Look at the spot between the person's upper eyelid and eyebrow.
It's called the eye cover fold. When someone really enjoys something,
that part of the face moves slightly down.
It's very hard to fake.

✳

Keep them talking. The more a person says,
the more chance they have to lose control over the lie.

✳

As they throw the wrapping paper into the fire or trashcan,
look carefully to see if your gift goes with it.

HOW MANY IS TOO MANY?

Seconds you wash your hands in the men's room: **5**

Number of times you roll up your sleeves: **5**

Seconds you ask to be held back before you realize
your friends aren't going to help you get out of this fight: **1**

Pairs of underwear you pack for a weekend getaway: **4**

Seconds you search for the quarter you dropped on the street: **2**

Dollar bills: **10**

Seconds you peruse the menu before deciding what to order: **30**

TV shows you watch regularly: **4**

Games of pool you play before giving up the table: **4**

Exclamation marks you use in a text: **1**

Seconds you hold the kiss at your wedding: **3**

Seconds you look at a tattoo before commenting: **3**

Number of items on this list: **14**

CHAPTER TEN

TROUBLE-SHOOTING

WHAT I'VE LEARNED

My father would say, "Do the best you can. And then the hell with it." He always looked at the effort grade rather than the final grade.

—TED KENNEDY

I can tell a young person where the mines are, but he's probably going to have to step on them anyway.

—BURT REYNOLDS

THE RULES

RULE NO. 977:
There's no reason to ever say "whoops" out loud.

RULE NO. 983:
Love does not mean never having to say you're sorry. It means having to say you're sorry over and over again, in new and different ways, every day, every week, every month, every year, until God grants you his mercy and you finally, blissfully die.

THE LANGUAGE OF DISTRESS

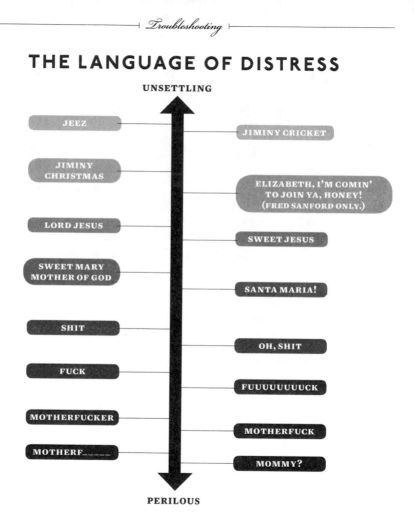

YOU'VE BEEN CAUGHT

-STEP 1-

SHOW VULNERABILITY IMMEDIATELY. If you're defenseless, people are much less likely to attack you. Drop your hands. Don't bring the guns. Don't fight a war that you don't want to win.

-STEP 2-

CHOOSE YOUR WORDS CAREFULLY. You made a mistake. You strayed and crossed the line. (You did not "cheat.") You want to know what you can do to get a second chance. (Everyone knows in the back of their mind that people deserve second chances. This is better than talking about "staying together" or "not leaving.")

-STEP 3-

OFFER TO ATONE. "What can I do to make this right?" Because you need to plant the seed in her mind that this situation can, in fact, be made right.

-STEP 4-

IF THERE ARE KIDS INVOLVED, DON'T BRING THEM INTO IT OR USE THEM AS COLLATERAL IN YOUR NEGOTIATIONS. This will only piss her off.

-STEP 5-

KEEP HER IN THE ROOM. The longer you're in the same room after you've been caught, the greater the chance you have of working it out. Instead of telling her everything right away, ask her what she wants to know, and let her drive the conversation. She will check everything you say, so don't lie.

THE EVERYMAN'S GUIDE TO

NOTABLE TRANSGRESSIONS

....

HEY: IT COULD HAPPEN TO ANYONE.

....

❶
YOU'VE CAUSED SOME TROUBLE ON A PLANE AND YOU'VE BEEN ASKED TO STEP OFF. No good arguing with Charlene or whoever has asked you to step off—they've got all the power, and an escalating war of words will not end in your favor. Either apologize profusely and ask to be let back on the plane, or simply go to the ticket counter, calmly explain the situation, and request a ticket on the next flight. You won't be treated like a criminal unless you act like one. Once you're on that second flight, you're just a regular passenger again.

②

**YOU'RE BEING
CALLED A RACIST
BECAUSE OF A
STUPID JOKE.**
Do not lead with
"Lighten up."
Condescension will
get you nowhere. Make
clear that you know you
said something stupid
and offensive—use the
word *stupid* as many
times as possible—and
that you get why they're
offended. Say you're
sorry and leave race
jokes to Chris Rock.

③

**CATFISH'D!
(OR, AT THE VERY
LEAST, HOAXED.)**
Take inventory of
everything you shared
with the scammer—
photos, personal

information, your hopes
and dreams. If you sent
money, call the cops. If
they try to blackmail
you (with compromising
photos or embarrassing
personal details), call
the cops. If it doesn't
involve money—only
your pride—there's no
legal solution. Cut off all
contact and block them
from your social-media
profiles.

④

**YOU'VE TWEETED
A, AHEM, REVEALING
PHOTO.**
Delete the offending
tweet ASAP, and do not
run around saying your
account was hacked by
someone in possession
of vintage photos of
Mark Wahlberg in
the Funky Bunch era.

You're busted. Find your
significant other and
'fess up before she sees
it herself and imagines
the worst.

⑤

**YOU'VE BEEN
CAUGHT IN
AN EXTRAVAGANT
LIE.**
Stop lying. You'll have
only one shot to come
clean with friends and
family. Explain why you
lied, making sure you
acknowledge you are
offering an explanation,
not an excuse, and hope
for empathy. Then shift
your focus to making
amends through
actions, not words. ("I
will do [insert action]
to make this right," and
then do it.)

YOU'VE BEEN ARRESTED

➤ **KEEP YOUR MOUTH SHUT** and wait for your lawyer. However: Don't refuse to answer simple booking information (name, address, DOB). That will force the officers to book you as John Doe and only lengthen the process.

➤ **NEVER TELL A POLICE OFFICER** what he can't do (e.g., "You can't lock me up"). Because he can do a lot, and nothing guarantees he will do it more than you telling him he can't.

➤ **DON'T DROP NAMES.** Cops don't care that your Uncle Paul is best friends with the police commissioner. (If, however, your Uncle Paul *is* the commissioner, there's no harm in letting that be known.)

➤ **DON'T RESIST ANYTHING,** especially if you're in for something involving violence. Should you choose not to go with the flow, you can tack on resisting arrest (or some such) to your existing charges.

➤ **DON'T MAKE DEMANDS.** You will get your phone call, but usually it has to wait until all the paperwork is done. And if you're nice, you might even get two calls.

➤ **CALL SOMEONE** who can carry the ball (access money for bail, know whom to call to get you a lawyer after you hang up). This may or may not be your wife. Choose wisely.

➤ **GET YOURSELF A CRIMINAL ATTORNEY**—not a friend who is a corporate attorney. If you don't know one, start with a court-appointed lawyer. It's always better than not having one at all, and most of them are highly qualified.

IT'S SUNNY AND

YOU NEED TO TAKE A PICTURE

◆ Shoot in the late afternoon, when the light is softer and you get more pleasing, sculpting shadows.

◆ Stand between the sun and what you're shooting. Ideally, the sun should be at your back, about 30 degrees off to one side.

◆ If you're on the beach and you have a dark blanket, lay it in front of your subject (out of the shot) to cut down on reflected light.

◆ For a moodier look, close your aperture one to two stops, making the background more of a blur.

With thanks to Michael Dweck, photographer, whose work includes the books Habana Libre and The End: Montauk, N.Y. and the photo above.

◆ Make sure your subject's hands are doing something. Even something simple like swinging, brushing hair, or holding a beer.

THE BEFORE AND AFTER OF

GOOD POSTURE

BEFORE

SLOUCHING SQUEEZES the spinal disks and increases core muscle tension, both of which lead to muscle fatigue. It also makes you look meek.

AFTER

LIFT THE STERNUM, let the shoulders slide back slightly, keep chin level. Maintain and run for president someday.

THE GOOD-POSTURE WALL EXERCISE

1. Stand with your head, shoulders, and back against a wall.

2. Position your feet about six inches away from the wall.

3. Flatten your back against the wall while maintaining the fixed position of your feet. Ignore stares of passersby.

4. Push away from the wall by arching your lower back while keeping your shoulders and head against the wall.

5. Repeat movement 10 to 15 times twice a day.

THE **SOCIAL DILEMMA**

YOUR PARTY
GUESTS
WON'T LEAVE

❶

Subtly taper off
the entertainment.
Gather glasses and
bottles and put away
any remaining food.

❷

Start loading the
dishwasher. Yawn
and say, "Honey we
should really go to
bed. These people
want to get going."

❸

Openly use cleaning
products. Ask them
to help by taking out
the trash. Or going
out and getting in
their car.

THE WORST-CASE SCENARIO

GUIDE TO ENTERTAINING

THE FOUL	THE FIX
YOU'VE BURNED DINNER.	If you've burned soup, stew, or sauce, they're lost causes; if you've burned chicken or steak, simply cut away the offending burned skin or gently scrape off the charred crust using the back of a knife, then serve; if you've burned rice or pasta dishes, remove the burned layer(s) and serve the rest.
A GUEST HAS SPILLED WINE ON YOUR CARPET.	Blot up as much as you can, and then, using a clean white cloth, apply a solution of one tablespoon dish soap, one tablespoon white vinegar, and two cups warm water. Blot with a dry cloth until the stain disappears, and then sponge with cold water and blot dry.
SOMEONE STARTS CHOKING.	Stay calm! Wrap your arms around the choker's waist, make a first, and place the thumb side of your fist against her upper abdomen below the rib cage around the navel. Grasp your fist with your other hand and thrust into the upper abdomen until she is able to breathe. Allow her to thank you for saving her life.
A DRUNKEN FISTFIGHT BREAKS OUT.	Drunk people don't listen and don't care whom they hit, so the last thing you want to do is get in the middle of it and risk a broken nose (or worse). Instead, grab the nearest glass (or, better, pitcher) of ice water and douse the more aggressive of the two in the face. Repeat until he snaps out of it and comes to his senses.

HOW TO **COMPLAIN EFFECTIVELY**

SOMETHING WILL GO WRONG: A ZIPPER WON'T ZIP
OR A SEAM WILL TEAR WIDE OPEN. SOME POINTERS
ON GETTING THE MOST OUT OF A COMPLAINT.

❶

Stay cool and understand that it's probably not the frontline
employee's fault. Ask to speak to a manager.

❷

Get the manager to appreciate where you're coming from.
Tell him your story. Tell him what, specifically, about the product
or experience wasn't satisfying—saying you just didn't like
something makes you sound like a pisser and/or moaner.

❸

Don't give up. If he says there's nothing he can do to help you, say:
"Look, I understand where you're coming from, and I've really liked doing
business with you in the past. Is there anyone else I can talk to about this?"
And then you might have someone who actually goes to bat for you and
says, "I got a really nice guy out here. What can we do for him?"

❹

Learn your lesson. If the service provider has really messed up
but can't help you (or simply chooses not to), take your business elsewhere.

THE
BIG BLACK BOOK
EXCUSE
GENERATOR

SEVEN FAIL-PROOF EXCUSES TO GIVE WHEN A FRIEND ASKS TO STAY AT YOUR PLACE. (START EACH WITH "YOU KNOW I WOULD, BUT . . .")

"...we're out of town that night. Damn!"

"...the in-laws are here."

"...the kids are sick, and now my wife's got it. A festival of germs, this place."

"...getting rid of bedbugs is even more involved than they would have you believe."

"...the wife and I are working through some things. Nothing too serious, but we need a little time."

"...we're remodeling the bathroom. It's not a big deal, it's just that we'll all have to shower at the gym."

"...I may still have feelings for your wife."

CHAPTER ELEVEN

THE QUIZ!

ARE YOU A "MAN"?

There is such a thing as being too much of a man—a hyperbolic oaf driven primarily by base desire, ego, and beer. While you are welcome to be such a man, especially if you are a sailor in the 1950s, you should at least do so with a bit of self-awareness. Now that you've read through this book, let's find out where you stand in the landscape of masculine virtues—competence, emotional and physical discipline, self-possession, honesty, humor, and a solid first name of at least two and no more than three syllables. (Pro tip: You don't have to do too well on this one.)

1. 'Sup.
  a. 'Sup. (1)
  b. Hi! (-1)

2. Is your name Chase, Blake, Noah, or Jayden?
  a. Yes (-5)
  b. No (5)

3. How about Channing?
  a. Yes (-6)
  b. No (0)

4. How old are you?
  a. Younger than 41. (1)
  b. Older than 41. (1)
  c. I'm 41. (-5)

5. Complete this sentence: "What the ____?"
  a. hell (4)
  b. fuck (5)
  c. shit (6)
  d. motherfuck (7)
  e. Christ (8)

7. How skinny do you like your ties?

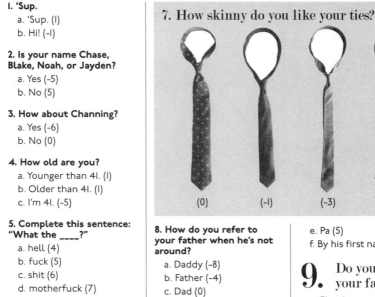

(0)   (-1)   (-3)   (5)

6 Which Malcom Gladwell photo makes you angriest?

(1)   (2)   (3)

8. How do you refer to your father when he's not around?
  a. Daddy (-8)
  b. Father (-4)
  c. Dad (0)
  d. Pops (3)
  e. Pa (5)
  f. By his first name (10)

9. Do you hate your father?
  a. Eh, it's complicated. (1)
  b. Love the guy. (-5)

10. The Brewers (-105, +1.5) are playing the Reds (-115, -1.5). Gallardo against Arroyo. What do you say?
  a. Take Gallardo at 1.5 and Milwaukee. (1)
  b. Give 1.5 and take Cincy. (2)
  c. Pardon me? (-2)

11. Which setting is your Google "SafeSearch" currently set to?

a. "Strict" (5)
b. "Moderate" (-3)
c. "Off" (2)

12. How quickly could you bed a woman if you began the attempt right now?

a. I am already in bed with a woman. (8)
b. Within 30 minutes. (6)
c. Within 24 hours. (0)
d. Gimme a month. (-4)
e. Do you know anyone? (-6)

13. Have you ever used the phrase "bed a woman"?

a. Yes (-5)
b. No (2)

14. Do you have long hair?

a. Yes (-5)
b. No (0)

15. If you answered "yes," are you a Samoan?

a. Yes (10)
b. No (-3)
c. I do not have long hair. (-5)

16. How many restraining orders are currently filed against you?

a. 0 (0)
b. More than 0 (-10)

17. Which word do you enjoy saying more?

a. Asshole (7)
b. Schmuck (8)

18. Which one is S.I. Swimsuit Issue model Kate Upton and which is S.I. Swimsuit Issue model Brooklyn Decker?

a. Upton on the left, Decker on the right.
b. Decker on the left, Upton on the right.
c. They are both Kate Upton.
d. They are both Brooklyn Decker.

19. Say you're in the market for replacement mud flaps. Which would you choose?

(0)   (3)   (5)

20. Are you at all involved in NBC's Thursday-night lineup in any sort of creative way?

a. Yes (-5)
b. No (0)
c. Yes, but I'm Alec Baldwin. (-2)

21. Doesn't matter.

a. Oh, really. (-5)

Honestly, we have no idea, either. But give yourself 5 points for trying.

22. Describe the pattern on the shirt you are currently wearing.

  a. Gingham (-5)

  b. Not gingham (5)

23. Have you ever in your life used the term "my own bare hands"?

  a. Yes (3)

  b. No (0)

24. You see that woman over there?

  a. Yes (2)

  b. No (-2)

25. She keeps looking over at you.

  a. Nah, she's looking at someone else. (-5)

  b. Nice. I'm going over. (5)

26. Have you ever witnessed the butchering of a whole hog?

  a. Yes (5)

  b. No (0)

27. Say you have a gopher in your yard. Which method would you use to discourage it?

  a. A humane trap for relocating it to a more appropriate habitat. (1)

  b. Let the dog at it! (3)

  c. Smoke it on out! (4)

  d. Flood it! (5)

  e. Put a .204 Ruger on it! (6)

  f. What you want to do is, feel around in there and pull it on out. (What the hell?)

28. In what way do you mitigate the transfer of germs when exiting the restroom at work?

  a. I touch a part of the door that I doubt other men touch (-2)

  b. I protect my hand with a paper towel (-3)

  c. I use a body part other than my hand to open the door. (-6)

  d. Isn't that what skin is for? (5)

29. Have you heard any song from the album Swanlights by the band Antony and the Johnsons, even if by accident?

  a. Yes (-2)

  b. No (2)

30. How near are you to a copy of the best-selling novel Sing You Home, by Jodi Picoult?

  a. Why, I have one right here! (-5)

  b. My wife occasionally reads passages of it to me in bed. (-3)

  c. I let my cousin borrow it. (-7)

  d. I don't know what you're talking about (5)

31. How many of the following publications have you recently looked to for guidance on "how to be a man"? (Check all that apply.)

  a. *The Ultimate Man's Survival Guide: Recovering the Lost Art of Manhood* (Regnery, 2009) (-4)

  b. *Man Up! 367 Classic Skills for the Modern Guy* (Artisan, 2011) (-2)

  c. *The Modern Gentleman, Second Edition: A Guide to Essential Manners, Savvy & Vice* (Ten Speed Press, 2011) (-6)

  d. *This book* (-2)